Ethereum: An Almost Complete Blueprint to Understanding and Profiting with Ethereum
By Florino Alfeche

© Copyright 2017 - All rights reserved.

This document, as presented, with the desire to provide reliable, quality information about the topic in question and the facts discussed within. This eBook is sold under the assumption that neither the author nor the publisher should be asked to provide the services discussed within. If any discussion, professional or legal, is otherwise required a proper professional should be consulted.

This Declaration was held acceptable and equally approved by the Committee of Publishers and Associations as well as the American Bar Association.

The reproduction, duplication or transmission of any of the included information is considered illegal whether done in print or electronically. Creating a recorded copy or a secondary copy of this work is also prohibited unless the act of doing so is first cleared through the Publisher and condoned in writing. All rights reserved.

TABLE OF CONTENTS
   CHAPTER 1
- Introduction
- What is Ethereum?
- Comparing Bitcoin and Ethereum
- The Future of Bitcoin and Ether
- Recommended Investment Strategy
- Projected Returns of the 5 Year Investment

   CHAPTER 2
- A NEXT GENERATION BLOCKCHAIN
- Ethereum Virtual Machine
- Learn about Ethereum
- How to use this guide?

- Using Ethereum: The Basics
- Web 3: A platform for decentralized apps
- Smart contracts
- DAO
- History of Ethereum
- The Ethereum Foundation and the ether presale
- ETH/DEV and Ethereum development
- The Ethereum Foundation

CHAPTER 3
- Ethereum Tools
- Acquiring the Virtual Machine
- Installing Pyethereum and Serpent
- The Smart-Contract Programming Model
- 4 Simulating Contracts with Pyethereum Tester
- Public and Private Keys
- Language Reference
- The log() Function
- Variables
- Control Flow
- Random Number Generation

CHAPTER 4
- Peer-to-peer (P2P)
- Introducing Swap
- Peer Protocol
- Indexer Protocol
- Oracle Protocol
- Smart Contract

CHAPTER 5
- A NEXT GENERATION SMART CONTRACT & DECENTRALIZED APPLICATION PLATFORM
- Merkle Trees Alternative Blockchain Applications
- Code Execution
- Financial derivatives and Stable-Value Currencies
- Identity and Reputation Systems
- Decentralized File Storage
- Decentralized Autonomous Organizations
- Further Applications
- Modified GHOST Implementation
- Currency And Issuance
- Issuance Breakdown

- Mining Centralization
- Scalability
- Putting It All Together: Decentralized Applications

CHAPTER 6
- Transactions
- Timestamp Server
- Proof-of-Work
- Network
- Incentive
- Reclaiming Disk Space
- Simplified Payment Verification
- Combining and Splitting Value
- Privacy
- Calculations
- Recommendation
- Conclusion

CHAPTER 1
Introduction

With ubiquitous internet connections in most places of the world, global information transmission has become incredibly cheap. Technology-rooted movements like Bitcoin have demonstrated, through the power of the default, consensus mechanisms and voluntary respect of the social contract that it is possible to use the internet to make a decentralized value-transfer system, shared across the world and virtually free to use. This system can be said to be a very specialized version of a cryptographically secure, transaction-based state machine. Follow-up systems such as Name coin adapted this original \currency application" of the technology into other applications albeit rather simplistic ones.

Ethereum is a project which attempts to build the generalized technology; technology on which all transaction-based state machine concepts may be built. Moreover, it aims to provide to the end-developer a tightly integrated end-to-end system for building software on a hitherto unexplored Computer paradigm in the mainstream: a trustful object messaging compute framework.

What is Ethereum?
Ethereum is an open blockchain platform that lets anyone build and use decentralized applications that run on blockchain technology. Like Bitcoin, no one controls or owns Ethereum – it is an open-source project built by many people around the world. But unlike the Bitcoin protocol, Ethereum was designed to be adaptable and flexible. It is easy to create new applications on the Ethereum platform, and with the Homestead release, it is now safe for anyone to use those applications.

Comparing Bitcoin and Ethereum
In order to choose an investment strategy between Bitcoin and Ethereum, it is important to understand the characteristics that differentiate the two cryptocurrencies. Bitcoin was first released on January 3rd, 2009 while Ethereum's live blockchain was initially launched on July 30th, 2015. Both of these cryptocurrencies are exchanged by using blockchain technology. A blockchain is a public ledger of all transactions that have occurred. Blocks are added in a linear chronological order. The ledger is public because each node has the full blockchain so it cannot be falsified by a single entity.

A node is any computer that is connected to the blockchain and used to execute and verify transactions (Investopedia, 2016). Although each uses blockchain technology they have different goals in mind, which can be seen through the coding protocols put in place.
Bitcoin was designed to act as a secure peer to peer decentralized payment system. Since everything is shown on the public ledger, the blockchain, you can be confident that the transaction is legitimate and the need to trust the other party is negated. Security is Bitcoin's first priority followed by speed. A Bitcoin transaction will show up in as little as one hour and is very secure due to the coding language used.
Bitcoin uses C++ programming and has less than 70 specific commands that can be used. This limitation provides more security because it is much more difficult to hack the blockchain within those set commands (Demeester, 2016).

Bitcoins are put into circulation by mining. Mining is "is the process of adding transaction records to Bitcoin's public ledger of past transactions or blockchain" (Hesoid Services LLC, 2016). Miners' processing power is used to complete transactions, and an incentive to do so they are rewarded Bitcoin. The current reward is 25 Bitcoin per block; this reward halves every 210,000 blocks. The next halving is expected to take place in 2020. There will be a finite amount of Bitcoins created; the maximum is 21,000,000 (Janin, Ethereum for Investors Part I, 2015).

Bitcoin operates on a proof-of-work basis. Proof-of-work means that in order to create blocks and add them to the blockchain you must solve very complex mathematical problems. This ensures that the information was difficult and costly to make, which helps to prevent fraud and malicious activity because of the cost involved in creating the block. The proof-of-work model, while it does help to increase security and validity, does have some negative effects.

First, it does not give miners an incentive to collaborate and they don't have anything at stake which means there is no consequence for malicious activity (Janin, Ethereum For Investors Part II, 2015). The second problem with proof-of-work is the amount of energy required to validate transactions. Many people consider this "wasted energy" and feel it has a negative impact on the environment. Now that we have an understanding of Bitcoin, let's look at the characteristics of Ethereum and show how it differs from Bitcoin.

Ethereum was designed to be much more than a payment system. It is "a decentralized platform that runs smart contracts: applications that run exactly as programmed without any possibility of downtime, censorship, fraud or third party interference." (Ethereum Foundation, 2016). Ethereum's protocol is built to allow flexibility and increase functionality to provide the ability to program many different types of smart contracts within the Ethereum system. Ethereum is written in Turing complete language, which includes seven different programming languages. We'll note that this is very different from Bitcoin, which is written in C++.

When Ethereum was launched they had an initial offering of ether (the cryptocurrency behind Ethereum). The sale of around 60 million ether resulted in raising around $18.5 million (Ethereum community, 2016). Additional ether is released via the mining process, similar to Bitcoin. The reward per block is 5 ether and remains constant, it does not halve. Also contrary to Bitcoin, Ethereum does not have a maximum total number of ether but does cap the amount released each year. Ethereum block times are currently at about 14 seconds, compared to Bitcoin's 10 minutes.

Ethereum also currently operates on a proof-of-work basis. Miners are rewarded for processing transactions and executing smart contracts, which create blocks. Ethereum is currently working towards changing to a proof-of-stake model which will change the reward system dramatically. As we discussed earlier, proof-of-work does not encourage collaboration nor does it provide any consequence for the malicious behavior. Proof-of-stake will change that.

In a proof-of-stake model there will no longer be miners, but validators. There will no longer be cryptographic challenges, the difficult mathematical problems that miners must solve. Validators will be required to own ether and in order to validate a block, they will be required to put their owned ether on the line to certify that a block is valid. This way, if there is malicious behavior or a validator does something invalid they will lose their stake, their owned ether.

Another difference will be the method of reward. Instead of rewarding miners for creating blocks validators will earn a transaction fee for each transaction and the smart contract they validate. This will be much more energy efficient and will put a focus on bandwidth rather than hash rate (number of calculations per second).

It will also help to put the focus on collaboration rather than the competition because the faster everyone can reach consensus (which is necessary to complete a block) the more transactions they'll be able to complete, resulting in higher profits (Janin, Ethereum For Investors Part II, 2015). The parties that want the transaction or smart contract executed will also pay a fee (called the gas price) in order to have it completed and added to the blockchain.

In summary, there are many differences that make Bitcoin and Ethereum distinct from one another. We do not believe that they have an inverse relationship, meaning when one increases in value, the other decreases; they can coexist as they are working towards different goals.

Bitcoin is striving to provide fast and secure transactions while Ethereum is focusing on much more. As more and smarter contracts and decentralized applications are built Ethereum's popularity and profitability will increase. Although both are volatile at this point, ether is so new that it is difficult to predict where it will go. We believe that both of these cryptocurrencies have benefits and will see an increase in value going forward.

The Future of Bitcoin and Ether

As we look to the future, we expect Bitcoin to continue to make strides to become an accepted currency worldwide. According to Coinbase, one of the largest Bitcoin exchanges, around 20 percent of activity on its network was payment related rather than speculative investment in January 2016 (Metz, 2016). While that percentage may seem small, it is growing as Bitcoin becomes more accepted as a currency.

One thing the public expects from a currency is being able to easily spend it. Bitcoin made strides in that area when Coinbase introduced the country's first bitcoin debit card. The company reported that more than 7,500 people signed up for the card within two months of its launch (Metz, 2016). In addition to making it easier for users to spend their Bitcoin, it will also help push more businesses to accept Bitcoin. By accepting Bitcoin outright, they can benefit from lower service fees than from the Bitcoin debit card.

In April 2016, another important step toward the legitimacy of Bitcoin occurred when Bitstamp, a Bitcoin exchange, was granted a payment institution license in Luxembourg. This license allows Bitstamp to operate in all European Union countries under the EU's "passport" program. According to the exchange's co-founder and chief executive Nejc Kodrič, "'[w]e believe that this is stability-inducing — that people will see this as a sign of Bitcoin going mainstream'" (Shin, 2016). The recognition of Bitcoin as a true currency by European governments will only encourage more people to utilize it. This will increase demand and therefore the currency's value.

In addition to being used as a currency, Bitcoin's blockchain technology is being utilized in other ways. "[A] group of tech and finance giants—IBM, Intel, Cisco, the London Stock Exchange Group, JP Morgan, Wells Fargo, and others—teamed up to create Hyperledger, an open source project inspired by Bitcoin that the companies hope will one day provide a more secure and reliable way of trading stocks and other assets" (Finley, 2016). For example, IBM says that disputes over tax rates or incorrect shipments take an average of 40 days to resolve today. With Hyperledger, the hope is this process can be streamlined (2016). Such large, reputable companies utilizing Bitcoin's blockchain technology will help to increase the currency's acceptance.

Due to these factors, we anticipate Bitcoin moving into a period of greater stability and adoption as a currency. This will continue to result in growth, but not at the breakneck speed of earlier years. However, it will not have the volatility of its infancy either.

On the contrary, the future of the currency ether depends upon Ethereum's technology being used. Ethereum made great strides in having its technology accepted as the blockchain standard when Microsoft Azure started offering it as a service in November 2015. Microsoft indicated it chose Ethereum over Bitcoin because "[w]hile a platform like Bitcoin has many great uses specifically as a Cryptocurrency, Ethereum provides the flexibility and extensibility many of our customers were looking for" (Gray, 2015). By offering Ethereum as part of Azure,

Microsoft is making the technology available to far more users than would otherwise use it. This will help to spur further innovations.

One industry that is already developing many uses for Ethereum is the Internet of Things (IoT). For example, the Ethereum computer could unlock doors when someone rents an office or apartment space (Tual, 2016). As more and more devices are connected to the Internet, the ability for them to interact with one another by using Ethereum's smart contracts becomes ever more valuable. In fact, IBM believes that blockchain technology is key to the success of IoT. In a time when over a billion devices could be connected to the internet, "the blockchain is the framework facilitating transaction processing and coordination among interacting devices. Each manages its own roles and behavior, resulting in an 'Internet of Decentralized, Autonomous Things' – and thus the democratization of the digital world" (IBM Institute for Business Value, 2015). Ethereum has a better technological foundation than Bitcoin does to take advantage of these needs.

Ethereum has many uses in the financial services industry as well. Nearly every bank currently uses SWIFT messaging to securely process transactions, but Ethereum smart contracts could cause this network to become archaic (Trivedi, 2016). Distributed ledgers could settle accounts more quickly and save banks, and therefore consumers, up to $20 billion a year (The great chain of being sure about things, 2015). This would also help to protect banks from the unethical actions of employees and the subsequent bad press.

There are risks with Ethereum's smart contracts as well. While smart contracts do not require consumers to trust each other, they do require them to trust the code. "[I]f code is law, so are bugs in the code—and correcting them may itself mean a breach of contract" (Not-so-clever contracts, 2016). While smart contracts are set up to be unchanging and trustworthy, they still ultimately are created by humans who are capable of error.

However, if Ethereum's smart contracts are utilized to the extent that we believe they will be, its currency Ether will be used more frequently as well and its value will subsequently increase. While the future of Ether is more uncertain than the future of Bitcoin, the potential gains are also much greater.

Figure 1: Number of Bitcoin Transactions Per Day

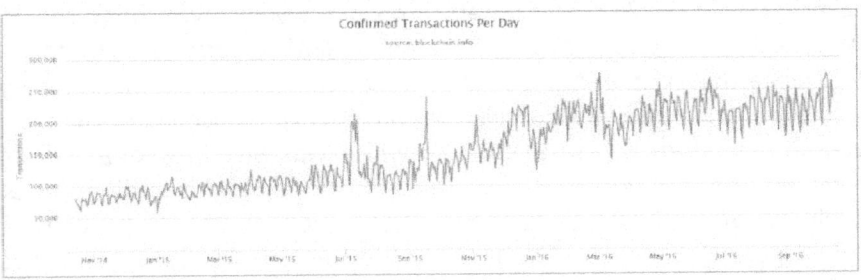

Source: blockchain.info, retrieved 10/12/16

Recommended Investment Strategy

The strategy we want to put in place for our investment is to limit our exposure to the downside risks associated with Ethereum but still be able to capture the upside potential. The future of Ethereum is all dependent on the progress of the smart contracts while Bitcoin's blockchain technology is very established. Therefore, our recommended structure for the $1,000,000 investment is to invest $700,000 into Bitcoin and $300,000 into Ethereum. Based on the last 12 months of return data for Ethereum and Bitcoin, we feel that the 70/30 investment is the max amount of risk we are willing to accept with Ethereum, where we can limit our risk with Ethereum but still have the upside to make a significant return (Figure 2).

Figure 2: Standard Deviation of Portfolio

Proportion of Ethereum	Variance of Portfolio	Portfolio Standard Deviation
0	0.022099282	14.87%
0.1	0.018875527	13.74%
0.2	0.03239462	18.00%
0.3	0.062656559	25.03%
0.4	0.109661344	33.12%
0.5	0.173408976	41.64%
0.6	0.253899455	50.39%
0.7	0.35113278	59.26%
0.8	0.465108952	68.20%
0.9	0.595827971	77.19%
1	0.743289837	86.21%

Projected Returns of the 5 Year Investment

The first step in projecting the return on our 5-year investment was to estimate the future annual growth rates for both Ethereum and Bitcoin. We believe that if Ethereum achieves their goals for the technology they could experience the same success that Bitcoin experienced early, and will have an annual growth rate 136.50% which was Bitcoin's compounded annual growth rate during the five years after one year of trading. As for Bitcoin, we are estimating a very conservative annual growth rate of 10%; as we Figure 1 demonstrates, Bitcoin's number of daily transactions has been steadily increasing over the past year, but we believe that these daily transactions may start to slow down if Ethereum achieves their goal. Another factor that leads to the conservative growth rate is our expectation that Ethereum will people able to capitalize on the smart contract technology, and this could ultimately cut into Bitcoin's market cap and swing the favor in Ethereum's direction. Based on our growth assumptions we project that one Ether will be worth $868.52 and one Bitcoin will be worth $988.74 at the end of the five year period (Figure 3).

Figure 3: Project Prices per unit (USD)

Projected Prices

	ETH	BTC
Current Price	$11.74	$613.93
Year 1	$27.76	$675.32
Year 2	$65.66	$742.86
Year 3	$155.29	$817.14
Year 4	$367.25	$898.85
Year 5	$868.52	$988.74

Assuming our recommended investment structure and projected future prices, our 5-year $1,000,000 investment will yield a total value of $22,321,145.06 or a return of 2232% (Figure 4).

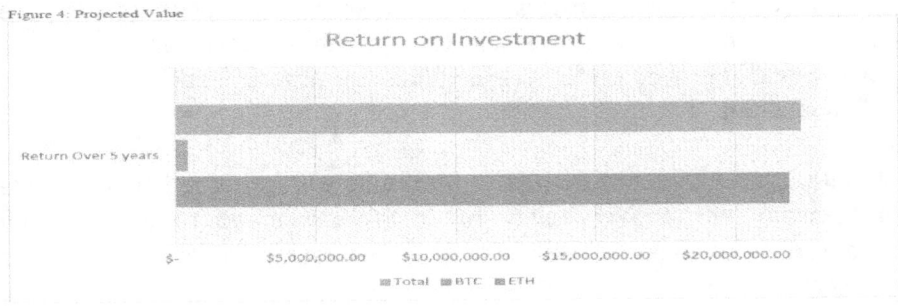

Figure 4: Projected Value

CHAPTER 2
A NEXT GENERATION BLOCKCHAIN

Blockchain technology is the technological basis of Bitcoin, first described by its mysterious author Satoshi Nakamoto in his white paper "Bitcoin: A Peer-to-Peer Electronic Cash System", published in 2008. While the use of blockchains for more general uses was already discussed in the original paper, it was not until a few years later that blockchain technology emerged as a generic term.

A blockchain is a distributed computing architecture where every network node executes and records the same transactions, which are grouped into blocks. Only one block can be added at a time, and every block contains a mathematical proof that verifies that it follows in sequence from the previous block.

In this way, the blockchain's "distributed database" is kept in consensus across the whole network. Individual user interactions with the ledger (transactions) are secured by strong cryptography. Nodes
That maintains and verify the network are incentivized by mathematically enforced economic incentives coded into the protocol.

In Bitcoin's case, the distributed database is conceived of as a table of account balances, a ledger, and transactions are transfers of the bitcoin token to facilitate trustless finance between individuals.

But as bitcoin began attracting greater attention from developers and technologists, novel projects began to use the bitcoin network for purposes other than transfers of value tokens. Many of these took the form of "altcoins" - separate blockchains with cryptocurrencies of their own which improved on the original Bitcoin protocol to add new features or capabilities.

In late 2013, Ethereum's inventor Vitalik Buterin proposed that a single blockchain with the capability to be reprogrammed to perform any arbitrarily complex computation could subsume these many other projects.
In 2014, Ethereum founders Vitalik Buterin, Gavin Wood and Jeffrey Wilcke began work on a next-generation blockchain that had the ambitions to implement a general, fully trustless smart contract platform.

Ethereum Virtual Machine
Ethereum is a programmable blockchain. Rather than give users a set of pre-defined operations (e.g. bitcoin transactions), Ethereum allows users to create their own operations of any complexity they wish. In this way, it serves as a platform for many different types of decentralized blockchain applications, including but not limited to cryptocurrencies.

Ethereum in the narrow sense refers to a suite of protocols that define a platform for decentralized applications.At the heart of it is the Ethereum Virtual Machine ("EVM"), which can execute code of arbitrary algorithmic complexity. In computer science terms, Ethereum is "Turing complete".

Developers can create applications that run on the EVM using friendly programming languages modeled on existing languages like JavaScript and Python. Like any blockchain, Ethereum also includes a peer-to-peer network protocol. The Ethereum blockchain databases maintained and updated by many nodes connected to the network. Each and every node of the network runs the EVM and executes the same instructions. For this reason, Ethereum is sometimes described evocatively as a "world computer".

This massive parallelization of computing across the entire Ethereum network is not done to make computation more efficient. In fact, this process makes computation on Ethereum far slower and more expensive than on traditional "computer". Rather, every Ethereum node runs the EVM in order to maintain consensus across the blockchain. Decentralized consensus gives Ethereum extreme levels of fault tolerance, ensures zero downtime, and makes data stored on the blockchain forever unchangeable and censorship-resistant. The Ethereum platform itself is featureless or value-agnostic. Similar to programming languages, it is up to entrepreneurs and developers to decide what it should be used for. However, it is clear that certain application types benefit more than others from Ethereum's capabilities. Specifically, there is suited for applications that automate direct interaction between peers or facilitate coordinated group action across a network. For instance, applications for coordinating peer-to-peer marketplaces, or the automation of complex financial contracts.

Bitcoin allows for individuals to exchange cash without involving any middlemen like financial institutions, banks, or governments. Ethereum's impact may be more far-reaching. In theory, financial interactions or exchanges of any complexity could be carried out automatically and reliably using code running on Ethereum. Beyond financial applications, any environments where trust, security, and permanence are important – for instance, asset-registries, voting, governance, and the internet of things – could be massively impacted by the Ethereum platform.

How does Ethereum work?
Ethereum incorporates many features and technologies that will be familiar to users of Bitcoin, while also introducing many modifications and innovations of its own.

Whereas the Bitcoin blockchain was purely a list of transactions, Ethereum's basic unit is the account.

The Ethereum blockchain tracks the state of every account, and all state transitions on the Ethereum blockchain are transfers of value and information between accounts. There are two types of accounts:

• Externally Owned Accounts (EOAs), which are controlled by private keys

• Contract Accounts, which are controlled by their contract code and can only be "activated" by an EOA

For most users, the basic difference between these is that human users control EOAs - because they can control the private keys which give control over an EOA. Contract accounts, on the other hand, are governed by their internal code. If they are "controlled" by a human user, it is because they are programmed to be controlled by an EOA with a certain address, which is in turn controlled by whoever holds the private keys that control that EOA. The popular term "smart contracts" refers to code in a Contract Account – programs that execute when a transaction is sent to that account. Users can create new contracts by deploying code to the blockchain.

Contract accounts only perform an operation when instructed to do so by an EOA. So it is not possible for contract account to be performing native operations like random number generation or API calls – it can do these things only if prompted by an EOA. This is because Ethereum requires nodes to be able to agree on the outcome of computation, which requires a guarantee of strictly deterministic execution.

Like in Bitcoin, users must pay small transaction fees to the network. This protects the Ethereum blockchain from frivolous or malicious computational tasks, like DDoS attacks or infinite loops. The sender of a transaction must pay for each step of the "program" they activated, including computation and memory storage.

These fees are paid in amounts of Ethereum's native value-token, ether. These transaction fees are collected by the nodes that validate the network. These "miners" are nodes in the Ethereum network that receive, propagate, verify, and execute transactions. The miners then group the transactions– which include many updates to the "state" of accounts in the Ethereum blockchain – into what are called "blocks", and miners then compete with one another for their block to be the next one to be added to the blockchain.

Miners are rewarded with ether for each successful block they mine. This provides the economic
The incentive for people to dedicate hardware and electricity to the Ethereum network. Just as in the Bitcoin network, miners are tasked with solving a complex mathematical problem in order to successfully
"Mine" a block. This is known as a "Proof of Work". Any computational problem that requires orders
of magnitude more resources to solve algorithmically than it takes to verify the solution is a good candidate for proof of work. In order to discourage centralization due to the use of specialized hardware (e.g. ASICs), as has occurred in the Bitcoin network, Ethereum chose a memory-hard computational problem. If the problem requires memory as well as CPU, the ideal hardware is, in fact, the general computer. This makes Ethereum's Proof of Work ASIC-resistant, allowing a more decentralized distribution of security than blockchains whose mining is dominated by specialized hardware, like Bitcoin.

Learn about Ethereum

[to be extended]

PR videos with some pathos:
- Ethereum: the World Computer
- Ethereum – your turn

Comparison to alternatives

- NXT
- MaidSafe

How to use this guide?
Using Ethereum: The Basics

This section captures the basic ways in which a user would want to participate in the Ethereum project. First of all becoming a node in the network, you need to run an Ethereum client. Multiple implementations are listed in the section choosing a client who also gives you advice what clients to choose in various setups. Connecting to the Network gives you basic information about networks, connectivity troubleshooting, and blockchain synchronization. Advanced network topics like setting up private chains are found in Test Networks.

The Homestead Release
Homestead is the second major version of the Ethereum platform and is the first production release of Ethereum. It includes several protocol changes and a networking change that provides the ability to do further network upgrades. The first version of Ethereum, called the Frontier release, was essentially a beta release that allowed developers to learn, experiment, and begin building Ethereum decentralized apps and tools.

Milestones of the Ethereum development roadmap
The original development roadmap laid out before Ethereum went live specified the following milestones:
- Prerelease Step 0: Olympic testnet - launched May 2015
- Release Step One: Frontier - launched 30 July 2015
- Release Step Two: Homestead - launches 14 March 2016 (Pi Day)
- Release Step Three: Metropolis - TBA
- Release Step Four: Serenity – TBA

While still valid, the substance behind it has changed somewhat. The Olympic testnet phase (before the Frontier release) saw a lot of major improvements, followed by Frontier which was launched immediately after. Homestead marks the exit from a beta product to a stable release. Homestead has introduced automatically at block number 1,150,000 which should occur roughly around March 14th, 2016, Pi Day.

If you are running a node connected to the live network, it is important that you upgrade to a Homestead compatible client. Such clients with their versions are listed under Ethereum Clients. Otherwise, you will end up on the wrong fork and will no longer be in sync with the rest of the network. Once the Ethereum blockchain reaches block 1,150,000, the Ethereum network will undergo a hard fork enabling a few major changes such as explained in the following section.

Homestead hard fork changes

Ethereum in the narrow formal sense is a suite of protocols. Homestead comes with a few backward-incompatible protocol changes, and therefore will require a hard fork.

These changes that made their way through the process for Ethereum Improvement Proposals and included are:

- **EIP 2:**
  - " Cost for creating contracts via a transaction is increased from 21000 to 53000. Contract creation from a contract using the CREATE opcode is unaffected.
  - " transaction signatures whose s-value is greater than secp256k1n/2 are now considered invalid— If contract creation does not have enough gas to pay for the final gas fee for adding the contract code to the state, the contract creation fails (ie. goes out-of-gas) rather than leaving an empty contract.
  - " Change the difficulty adjustment algorithm.

- **EIP 7:** DELEGATECALL: Add a new opcode, DELEGATECALL at 0xf4, which is similar in idea to CALLCODE, except that it propagates the sender and value from the parent scope to the child scope, ie. The call created has the same sender and value as the original call. This means contracts can store pass through

Information while following msg.sender and msg.value from its parent contract. Great for contracts which create contracts but don't repeat additional information which saves gas. See comments on EIP 7.

- **EIP 8**: devp2p Forward Compatibility compliance with the Robustness Principle Changes to the RLPx
Discovery Protocol and RLPx TCP transfer protocol to ensure that all client software in use on the Ethereum network can cope with future network protocol upgrades. For older versions of an Ethereum client, updates to the network protocol weren't being accepted by older clients and would refuse communication if the hello packets didn't meet expectations. This

update means all future versions of the client will accept incoming network upgrades and handshakes. The changes have the following benefits:

• **EIP-2/1** eliminates the excess incentive to create contracts via transactions, where the cost is 21000, rather than contracts, where the cost is 32000.

• EIP-2/1 also fixes the protocol "bug" that with the help of suicide refunds, it is currently possible to make a simple ether value transfer using only 11664 gas.

• EIP-2/2 fixes a transaction malleability concern (not a security flaw, but a UI inconvenience).

• EIP-2/3 creates a more intuitive "success or fail" distinction in the result of a contract creation process,
rather than the current "success, fail, or empty contract" trichotomy.

• EIP-2/4 eliminates the excess incentive to set the timestamp difference to exactly 1 in order to create a block that has slightly higher difficulty and that will thus be guaranteed to beat out any possible forks. This guarantee to keep block time in the 10-20 range and according to simulations restores the target 15-second block time (instead of the current effective 17s).

• EIP-7 makes it much easier for a contract to store another address as a mutable source of code and "pass through" calls to it, as the child code would execute in essentially the same environment (except for reduced gas and increased callstack depth) as the parent.

• EIP-8 makes sure that all client software in use on the Ethereum network can cope with future network protocol upgrades.

Additional resources: - Reddit discussion on Homestead Release - Ethereum Improvement Proposals (EIPs)

Web 3: A platform for decentralized apps
Many have come to believe that an open, trustless blockchain platform like Ethereum is perfectly suited to serve as the shared "back end" to a

decentralized, secure internet - Web 3.0. An internet where core services like DNS and digital identity are decentralized, and where individuals can engage in economic interactions with each other.

As intended by the Ethereum developers, Ethereum is a blank canvas and you have the freedom to build whatever you want with it. The Ethereum protocol is meant to be generalized so that the core features can be combined in arbitrary ways. Ideally, app projects on Ethereum will leverage the Ethereum blockchain to build solutions that rely on decentralized consensus to provide new products and services that were not previously possible.

Ethereum is perhaps best described as an ecosystem: the core protocol is supported by various pieces of infrastructure, code, and community that together make up the Ethereum project. Ethereum can also be understood by looking at the projects that use Ethereum. Already, there are a number of high-profile projects built on Ethereum such as Augur, Digix, Maker, and much more (see Dapps). In addition, there are development teams that build open source components that anyone can use. While each of these organizations are separate from the Ethereum Foundation and have their own goals, they undoubtedly benefit the overall Ethereum ecosystem.

Smart contracts
Would you enter into a contract with someone you've never met? Would you agree to lend money to some farmer in Ethiopia? Would you become an investor in a minority-run newspaper in a war zone? Would you go to the hassle of writing up a legal binding contract for a $5 dollar purchase over the internet?
The answer is no for most of these questions, the reason being that a contract requires a large infrastructure:
Sometimes you need a working trust relationship between the two parties, sometimes you rely on a working legal system, police force, and lawyer costs.

In Ethereum you don't need any of that: if all the requisites to the contract can be put in the blockchain then they will, in a trustless environment for almost no cost.
Instead of thinking of moving your current contracts to the blockchain, think of all the thousand little contracts that you would never agree to

simply because they weren't economically feasible or there was not enough legal protection.

DAO

Here is just one example: imagine you own a small business with your friends. Lawyers and accountants are expensive, and trusting a single partner to oversee the books can be a source of tension (even an opportunity for fraud). Complying strictly with a system in which more than one partner oversees the books can be trying and is subject to fraud whenever the protocol isn't followed exactly.

Using a smart contract, ownership in your company and terms for the disbursal of funds can be specified at the outset. The smart contract can be written such that it is only changeable given the approval of a majority of owners. Smart contracts like these will likely be available as open source software, so you won't even need to hire your own programmer instead of an accountant/lawyer.

A smart contract like this scales instantly. A couple of teenagers can split revenue from a lemonade stand just as transparently as a sovereign wealth fund can disburse funds to the hundred million citizens who are entitled to it.

In both cases, the price of this transparency is likely to be fractions of a penny per dollar.

History of Ethereum
Inception

Ethereum was initially described by Vitalik Buterin in late 2013 as a result of his research and work in the Bitcoin community. Shortly thereafter, Vitalik published the Ethereum white paper, where he describes in detail the technical design and rationale for the Ethereum protocol and smart contracts architecture. In January 2014, Ethereum was formally announced by Vitalik at The North American Bitcoin Conference in Miami, Florida, USA.

Around that time, Vitalik also started working with Dr. Gavin Wood and together co-founded Ethereum. By April 2014, Gavin published the Ethereum Yellow Paper that would serve as the technical specification for the Ethereum Virtual Machine (EVM). By following the detailed specification in the Yellow Paper, the Ethereum client has been implemented in seven programming languages (C++, Go, Python, Java, JavaScript, Haskell, Rust), and has resulted in better software overall.

- Ethereum launches Cryptocurrency 2.0 network - Coindesk article of 2014 Jan on the beginnings.
- Ethereum announcement on bitcointalk Vitalik's original announcement to the bitcoin community.

Forum thread with 5000 replies.

The Ethereum Foundation and the ether presale

In addition to developing the software for Ethereum, the ability to launch a new cryptocurrency and blockchain requires a massive bootstrapping effort in order to assemble the resources needed to get it up and running. To kickstart a large network of developers, miners, investors, and other stakeholders, Ethereum announced its plan to conduct a presale of ether tokens, the currency unit of Ethereum. The legal and financial complexities of raising funds through a presale led to the creation of several legal entities, including the Ethereum Foundation (Stiftung Ethereum) established June 2014 in Zug, Switzerland.

Beginning in July 2014, Ethereum distributed the initial allocation of ether via a 42-day public ether presale, netting 31,591 bitcoins, worth $18,439,086 at that time, in exchange for about 60,102,216 ether. The results of the sale were initially used to pay back mounting legal debts and also for the months of developer effort that had yet to be compensated and to finance the ongoing development of the Ethereum.

- Launching the ether sale - original official announcement on the Ethereum blog.
- Concise information-rich stats page about the presale by (since then inactive) Ether.Fund.
- Overview: Ethereum's initial public sale - Blog post by black nation - all stats about the ether presale.
- Terms and Conditions of the Presale.

ETH/DEV and Ethereum development

Following the successful ether presale, Ethereum development was formalized under a non-for-profit organization called ETH DEV, which manages the development of Ethereum under contract from Ethereum Suisse – with Vitalik Buterin, Gavin Wood, and Jeffrey Wilcke as the 3 directors of the organization. Developer interest in Ethereum grew steadily throughout 2014 and the ETH DEV team delivered a series of proof-of-concept (PoC) releases for the development community to evaluate. Frequent posts by ETH DEV team on the Ethereum blog also kept the excitement and momentum around Ethereum going. Increasing traffic and growing user-base on both the Ethereum forum and the ethereal subreddit testified that the platform is attracting a fast-growing and devoted developer community. This trend has been continuing to this very day.

DEVCON-0
In November 2014, ETH DEV organized the DEVCON-0 event, which brought together Ethereum developers from around the world to Berlin to meet and discuss a diverse range of Ethereum technology topics. Several of the presentations and sessions at DEVcon-0 would later drive important initiatives to make Ethereum more reliable, more secure, and more scalable. Overall, the event galvanized developers as they continued to work towards the launch of Ethereum.

- DEVCON-0 talks youtube playlist
- DEVCON-0 reddit post
- Gav's DEV update mentioning DEVCON-0
- DEVcon-0 recap blog post

DEVgrants program
In April 2015, the vagrant's program was announced, which is a program that offers to fund for contributions both to the Ethereum platform and to projects based on Ethereum. Hundreds of developers were already contributing their time and thinking to Ethereum projects and in open source projects. This program served to reward and support those developers for their contributions. The vagrant's program continues to operate today and funding of the program was recently renewed in January 2016.

- DEVgrants initial announcement
- Announcement of new funding at DEVCON-1
- DEVgrants public gitter room
- DEVgrants talk at DEVCON-1 by Wendell Davis on YouTube

Olympic testnet, bug bounty and security audit

Throughout 2014 and 2015 development went through a series of proof of concept releases leading to the 9th POC open testnet, called Olympic. The developer community was invited to test the limits of the network and a substantial prize fund was allocated to award those holding various records or having success in breaking the system in some way or other. The rewards were announced officially a month after the live release.

In early 2015, an Ethereum Bounty Program was launched, offering BTC rewards for finding vulnerabilities in any part of the Ethereum software stack. This has undoubtedly contributed to the reliability and security of Ethereum and the confidence of the Ethereum community in the technology. The bounty program is currently still active and there is no end date planned.

The Ethereum security audit began at the end of 2014 and continued through the first half of 2015. Ethereum engaged multiple third-party software security firms to conduct an end-to-end audit of all protocol-critical components (Ethereum VM, networking, Proof of Work). The audits uncovered security issues that were addressed and tested again and as a result ultimately led to a more secure platform.

- Olympic testnet prerelease - Vitalik's blogpost detailing olympic rewards
- Olympic rewards announced - Vitalik's blogpost detailing the winners and prizes
- Bug bounty program launch
- Ethereum Bounty Program website
- Least Authority audit blogpost - with links to the audit report
- Deja Vu audit blogpost

The Ethereum Frontier launch

The Ethereum Frontier network launched on July 30th, 2015, and developers began writing smart contracts and decentralized apps to deploy on the live Ethereum network. In addition, miners began to join the Ethereum network to help secure the Ethereum blockchain and earn either from mining blocks. Even though the Frontier release is the first milestone in the Ethereum project and was intended for use by developers as a beta version, it turned out to be more capable and reliable than anyone expected, and developers have rushed in to build solutions and improve the Ethereum ecosystem.

See also:
- Original announcement of the release scheme by Vinay Gupta
- Frontier is coming - Frontier launch announcement by Stephan Tual
- Frontier launch final steps - Follow-up post to announcement
- Ethereum goes live with Frontier launch
- The frontier website

DEVCON-1

The second developers' conference DEVCON-1 took place in the city of London at the beginning of November 2015. The 5-day event featured more than 100 presentations, panel discussions and lightning talks, attracted more than 400 participants, a mix of developers, entrepreneurs, thinkers, and business executives. The talks were all recorded and are freely available. The presence of large companies like UBS, IBM and Microsoft clearly indicated enterprise interest in the technology.

Microsoft announced that it would offer Ethereum on its new Blockchain as a Service offering on the
Microsoft Azure cloud platform. In conjunction with DEVCON-1, this announcement will be remembered as the moment when blockchain technology became mainstream, with Ethereum at the center of it.

- DEVCON-1 talks Youtube playlist.

- DEVCON-1 website full listing of presentations with links to the slides if available.

History resources
- A simple graphical timeline

Community
Please choose your forum wisely when starting a discussion or asking a question, help keep our various forums clean and tidy.

Reddit

The Ethereum subreddit is the most inclusive Ethereum forum, where most of the community discussion is happening and where core devs are also active. This is your forum of choice for generic discussion of news, media coverage, announcements, brainstorming. In general all things Ethereum relevant to the wider community. Strictly no price discussion.

Also, this is not the ideal place to ask for hands-on help or post questions you expect there are clear immediate answers to (use Gitter Rooms and Stack Exchange for these, respectively). Read the Ethereum subreddit rules before posting.

Further specialised subreddits:

- /r/EthTrader - Ether trading, price and market
- /r/EtherMining - Ether mining discussion
- /r/Ethmarket - Marketplace for individuals looking to exchange goods and services for Ether
- /r/Ethinvestor - News and prospects for Ethereum investors. Following the long term trends in the Ethereum marketplace.
- /r/ethereumism/ - A bit more ism, ostic, ical, ist and tinfoil hats, pyramids and crystal ball type of views -- the ethereal side of Ethereum.

Stack Exchange
The Ethereum Stack Exchange is part of the StackExchange network of Q&A communities. StackExchange is a free Q&A site where all the questions and answers are preserved for posterity.
This is the best place to ask technical questions. Help your fellow etherians by answering questions and collect reputation points.

Gitter Rooms
Gitter is our forum of choice for the daily chat. It is the virtual coworking space where devs hang out, so it is where you can get quick help and a bit of handholding if needed. Gitter uses Github accounts, offers Github integration (notification of pull requests etc), private channels, provides markdown formatting, and more.

Most Gitter channels are organized around particular repositories or generic topics like research or governance. Please choose the appropriate room and keep discussions on a topic. See the full list of glitter rooms for the Ethereum organization. Below is the list of active public channels:

- go-ethereum - about geth (and tools related to the go implementation)
- cpp-ethereum - about eth (and tools related to the C++ implementation)
- web3.js - about web3.js, Ethereum JavaScript API library
- Solidity - The Solidity Contract-Oriented Programming Language
- serpent - The Serpent language for contract development
- mist - GUI dapp browser, official wallet app
- light-client - about light client and the LES protocol
- research - Ethereum research
- governance - about dev governance
- whisper - anonymous datagram publishing
- swarm - decentralised content storage and distribution network
    - EIPs - discussion of Ethereum Improvement Proposals (EIPs)
    - ethereumjs-lib - a JavaScript library of core Ethereum functions
    - devp2p - Ð_V's p2p network protocol & framework

Ethereum Improvement Proposals (EIPs)

The EIP scheme aims to be a framework and largely informal business process coordinating improvements to the protocols. People should first propose their idea as an issue or pull request to the EIPs repository. After basic filtering, the proposal will receive a number and is published in draft form. For an EIP to become Active it will require the mutual consent of the community. Those proposing changes should consider that ultimately consent may rest with the consensus of the Ethereum users. For discussion of EIPs, use the gitter channel for EIP discussions.

- EIP guidelines and sample EIP
- EIP template
- EIP repository and README
- gitter channel for EIP discussions

Meetups

- Directory hosted on Meetup
- Meetup channel on Ethereum Forum

Obsolete

Skype

Some community discussion for still use skype rooms, but we would like to move away from that and encourage people to use gitter or slack.

Ethereum Forum

Stephan Tual's legendary Ethereum Forum is no longer maintained and likely to be decommissioned soon. We encourage people to use one of the recommended alternatives listed above.

The Ethereum Foundation

The Ethereum Foundation is a non-profit organization registered in Switzerland and has the purpose of managing the funds that were raised from the ether Sale in order to best serve the Ethereum and decentralized technology ecosystem.

Founded July 2014 in Switzerland, Stiftung Ethereum's mission is the promotion of developments of new technologies and applications, especially in the fields of new open and decentralized software architectures. It is the aim that decentralized and open technologies will be developed, nurtured, promoted and maintained. A dominating, but not exclusive, the focus is set on the promotion of the development of the Ethereum Protocol and the relevant technology to it as well as the promotion and support of applications using the Ethereum technology or protocol. Stiftung Ethereum will additionally support and advocate for a decentralized Internet in a variety of forms.

Ethereum Clients
Choosing a client
Why are there multiple Ethereum clients?

From the earliest days of the project, there have been multiple client implementations across a range of different operating systems. That client diversity is a huge win for the ecosystem as a whole. It lets us verify that the protocol (specified in the Yellow Paper) is unambiguous. It keeps the door open for new innovation. It keeps us all honest. However, it can be very confusing for end-users, because there is no universal "Ethereum Installer" for them to use.

As of September 2016, the leading implementations are go-ethereum and Parity.

Client	Language	Developers	Latest release
go-ethereum	Go	Ethereum Foundation	go-ethereum-v1.4.18
Parity	Rust	Ethcore	Parity-v1.4.0
cpp-ethereum	C++	Ethereum Foundation	cpp-ethereum-v1.3.0
pyethapp	Python	Ethereum Foundation	pyethapp-v1.5.0
ethereumjs-lib	Javascript	Ethereum Foundation	ethereumjs-lib-v3.0.0
Ethereum(J)	Java	<ether.camp>	ethereumJ-v1.3.1
ruby-ethereum	Ruby	Jan Xie	ruby-ethereum-v0.9.6
ethereumH	Haskell	BlockApps	no Homestead release yet

What should I install on my desktop/laptop?

Most users will likely just install Mist / Ethereum Wallet and that will be enough for their needs.

The Ethereum Wallet is a "single dapp" deployment of the Mist Browser which will be the centerpiece of the Metropolis phase of development, which comes after Homestead.

The mist comes with bundled go-ethereum and cpp-ethereum binaries and if you are not running a command-line Ethereum client when Mist starts then it will start syncing the blockchain using one of the bundled clients (defaulting to get).

If you want to use Parity with Mist, or to run Mist against a private network, just start your node before Mist, and Mist will connect to your node rather than starting one itself.

Work is underway to add Parity and other clients as "first-class entities" to Mist too.

If you want to interact with Ethereum on the command-line, and to take advantage of the Javascript console then you will want to install one of the client applications directly, as well as Mist.

Follow the links in the table above for further instructions.

If you want to do mining then Mist will not be sufficient.

Check out the Mining section.

What should I install on my mobile/tablet?

We are at the very beginning of our support for mobile devices. The Go team is publishing experimental iOS and Android libraries, which some developers are using to start bootstrapping mobile applications, but there are not yet any mobile Ethereum clients available.

The main hindrance to the use of Ethereum on mobile devices is that the Light Client support is still incomplete. The work which has been done is off in a private branch, and is only available for the Go client. Doublethinkco will be starting development of Light Client for the C++ client in the coming months, following grant funding.
Check out Status.im, who were initially using ethereumj-personal based on Ethereum(J), but have recently flipped to Geth cross-builds with Light Client.

What should I install on my SBC?
You have some choice here depending on your skill level, and what you are looking to do.

• Download a fully prepared image(link to page with detailed download & install instructions)
– If you are new to Ethereum AND SBC boards such as the Raspberry Pi then this is for you! Simply download the image specific to the dev board you are working with, burn it to an SD card, boot your device, and run Ethereum!

• Download a pre-compiled application (link to page with detailed download & install instructions)
– If you already have an SBC running and have a specific, preferred OS or setup that you want to keep, then this is your best option! Depending on the platform, you can simply download the appropriate executable, and with minimal linking of libraries and setting of PATH you can have Ethereum running in your existing environment!

• Build from source using customizable scripts (link to page with more detail and individual SBC. – Looking to perform a custom install? We have scripts available to compile from source "on device".

Our scripts contain auto-install of dependencies as well as the client itself. This will allow you to install a specific version of the Ethereum client(i.e.- "develop", "master", etc.), compile your own forked version of a client, and generally play around with the intracacies of the build process.

Interacting with Clients

In order to interact with Ethereum clients programmatically, please refer to the Connecting to Ethereum Clients section.

Quick Start

- Welcome to the Ethereum C++ project :-)
- The GitHub repository for this project is ethereum/cpp-ethereum
- Automation runs on Appveyor and TravisCI.
- We have instructions for Installing binaries and Building from source.
- Most project communication happens in our User and Developer Gitter channels.
- Issues are tracked in our Github issue tracker.
- cpp-ethereum is extremely portable and is used on a very broad range of platforms.

Details

Current status

We blog about the codebase periodically on the Official Ethereum blog and elsewhere. Here are some recent articles from the development team:

- Ethereum DEV Update: C++ Roadmap (February 2016)
- C++ DEV Update: Announcing Remix (May 2016)
- C++ DEV Update – July edition (July 2016)
- Ethereum Everywhere (July 2016)
- C++ re-licensing plan (July 2016)

We simplified the project naming at Homestead (March 2016), although some naming shadows of the past still linger. With the homecoming, we have another name to retire - webthree-umbrella.

At the time of writing (August 2016), we are just completing our "Homecoming", where the code has been reconsolidated into the ethereum/cpp-there repository. From October 2015 until August 2016 it was split across multiple repositories under ethereum/webthree-umbrella. The re-licensing plan is the culmination of a very long-term plan to liberalize the core. An effort was begun in 2015 to re-license the cpp-ethereum core as MIT, but it was never completed.

This is a revival of that effort, especially with a view towards the potential for collaboration with the Linux Foundation's Hyperledger project, and with other corporations outside of Hyperledger who wish to build Ethereum private/consortium chain solutions similar to HydraChain. The Rubix by Deloitte project is an example of that approach.

Building from source
Overview The cpp-ethereum codebase lives on Github.com in the cpp-ethereum repository.

Between October 2015 and August 2016 it was split into various repositories which were grouped as sub-modules under the webthree-umbrella repository, and you will likely see many references to webthree-umbrella online.

Those all refer to the cpp-ethereum codebase during that period of its development.

We use a common CMake build system to generate platform-specific build files, meaning that the workflow is very similar whatever operating system you use:

- Install build tools and external packages (these are platform dependent)
- Clone the source code from the webthree-umbrella git repository
- Run CMake to generate a build file (makefile, Visual Studio solution, etc)

- Build it

Platform-specific instructions
Building for Linux
Getting the source code we use git and GitHub to maintain the source code. Clone the repository by:

```
git clone --recursive https://github.com/ethereum/cpp-ethereum.git
cd cpp-ethereum
```

The --recursive option is important. It orders git to clone additional submodules which are required to build the project. If you missed it you can correct your mistake with command git submodule update --init. CMake We use CMake to control the build configuration of the project. Quite a recent version of CMake is required (at the time of writing 3.4 is the minimum). We recommend installing CMake by downloading and unpacking the binary distribution of the latest version available on the download page:https://cmake.org/download/

Alternative method
The repository contains the script install_cmake.sh that downloads a fixed version of CMake and unpacks it to the given directory prefix.

Example usage scripts/install_cmake.sh--prefix /usr/local.

Installing dependencies

The following libraries are required to be installed in the system:
- boost
- leveldb
- curl
- microhttpd
- miniupnp
- gmp

They usually can be installed using distribution-specific package manager. For example on Debian-based systems:

sudo apt-get install libboost-all-dev libleveldb-dev libcurl4-openssl-dev libmicrohttpd-dev libminiupnpc-or on RedHat-based systems:
dnf install boost-devel leveldb-devel curl-devel libmicrohttpd-devel miniupnpc-devel gmp-devel

Linux has a horror-show of fragmentation when it comes to packaging systems.
We support a "one-button" bash script which attempts to make this minefield more navigable for users of common distros. It identifies your distro and installs the external packages which you will need, using whatever combination of package servers and build-from-source is required for your specific distro version. This is a non-trivial task, but by that token is also something which we don't want anybody to have to replicate them. scripts/install_deps.sh

We use the same script for automated builds and continuous integration, so it is continuously tested, which is especially important on MacOS, where Homebrew is a constantly moving target. If you try it, and it doesn't work for you, please report the problem with details of your distro, your version number and any other important details and we can work together to get it working for your use-case.

We have manual instructions for Fedora, openSUSE, and Arch Linux (see below). If you using some other distro then please contact we and we'll see if we can get you going.

Installing dependencies for Fedora

Fedora 24 Steps:
dnf install git automake autoconf libtool cmake gcc gcc-c++ xkeyboard-config \ leveldb-devel boost-devel gmp-devel cryptopp-devel miniupnpc-devel \ qt5-qtbase-devel qt5-qtdeclarative-devel qt5-qtquick1-devel qt5-qtwebkit-devel \ mesa-dri-drivers snappy-devel ncurses-devel readline-devel curl-devel \ python-devel jsoncpp-devel argtable-devel libmicrohttpd-devel

Make sure you have cloned the repository recursively. If not please clone the submodules of the repository as well. It may happen that after # make install, you might not be able to run eth because of linking errors. In that case, you have to add the shared objects of eth into your load path for shared objects.

Installing dependencies for openSUSE
Here is how to get the dependencies needed to build the latest webthreeumbrella on OpenSUSE.

This was done on Leap 42.1 and 42.2, but there should be equivalent packages available for Tumbleweed and 13.x.

First install dependencies provided by the main repos:

```
zypper in git automake autoconf libtool cmake gcc gcc-c++ \
xkeyboard-config leveldb-devel boost-devel gmp-devel \
libcryptopp-devel libminiupnpc-devel libqt5-qtbase-common-devel \
libqt5-qtdeclarative-devel libQtWebKit-devel libqt5-qtwebengine-devel
\libQt5Concurrent-devel Mesa ncurses-devel readline-devel libcurl-devel
\llvm llvm-clang llvm-clang-devel llvm-devel libLLVM binutils \
         libmicrohttpd-devel jsoncpp-devel opencl-headers-1.2 zlib-devel
```

If Opencl-headers-1.2 is not found, you can install it manually from the CLI: zyppe addrepo
http://download.opensuse.org/repositories/home:valmar73:crystfelreleases/ openSUSE_13.1/home:valmar73:crystfel-releases.repo zypper refresh zypper install openclheaders-1.2

It may be possible to use the generic libOpenCL1, but I have only tested with the AMD proprietary package from the AMD drivers repo fglrx64_opencl_SUSE421
These packages are not in the standard repos but can be found using the OpenSUSE build service package search and YaST 1-Click Install:

- libargtable2-devel
- libv8-3
- v8-devel

If you also have v8 from the chromium repo installed the devel package will default to the 4.x branch which will not work. Use YaST or zypper to downgrade this package to 3.x
Note that Opencl-headers are used to mine the chain with GPU. If this is not a requirement, you can bypass it when creating the makefile (cmake -DETHASHCL=0 ..) instead of (cmake ..)

Installing dependencies for Arch Linux Compiling webthree-umbrella on Arch Linux requires dependencies from both the official repositories and the Arch User Repository (AUR). To install packages from the official repositories pacman is used. For installation of packages from the AUR, a number of AUR helpers are available. For this guide, yaourt AUR helper is used.

Installing dependencies # from official repositories sudo pacman -Sy git base-devel cmake boost crypto++ leveldb llvm miniupnpc libcl opencl-headers libmicrohttpd qt5-base qt5-webengine
from AUR yaourt -Sy libjson-rpc-cpp compiling the source code during this step, an installation folder for the Ethereum can be specified. Specification of the folder is optional though. If not given, the binary files will be located in the build folder. However, for this guide, it is assumed that the Ethereum files will be installed under /opt/eth. The reason for using /opt is that it makes much easier to delete the Ethereum files later on, as compared to having them installed under, e.g.,

/usr. Also /opt is commonly used to install software that is not managed by packaging systems, such as manually compiled programs.

enter webthree-umbrella folder after cloning its github repository cd webthree-umbrella

make a build folder and enter into it mkdir -p build && cd build

create build files and specify Ethereum installation folder

cmake .. -DCMAKE_INSTALL_PREFIX=/opt/eth

compile the source code make

alternatively it is possible to specify number of compilation threads

for example to use 4 threads execute make as follows:

make -j 4

install the resulting binaries, shared libraries and header files into /opt sudo make install

After successful compilation and installation, Ethereum binaries can be found in /opt/eth/bin, shared libraries in /opt/eth/lib, and header files in /opt/eth/include.

Specifying Ethereum libraries path Since Ethereum was installed in /opt/eth, executing its binaries can result in linker error due to not being able to find the Ethereum shared libraries. To rectify this issue, it is needed to add the folder containing Ethereum shared libraries into LD_LIBRARY_PATH environmental variable:

```
# update ~/.bashrc
echo "export LD_LIBRARY_PATH=$LD_LIBRARY_PATH:/opt/eth/lib" >> ~/.bashrc

# reload ~/.bashrc
source ~/.bashrc
```

Build on the command-line When you have installed your dependencies you can build.

```
mkdir build                    Make a directory for the build output
cd build                       Switch into that directory

cmake ..                       To generate a makefile.
make                           To build that makefile on the command-li
make -j<number>                (or) Execute makefile with multiple core
```

32-bit Linux builds We have cpp-ethereum building and running successfully on many 32-bit Linux distros, with the main constraint being the availability of external dependencies in 32-bit variants. Probably the most active demand here is for single-board computers like the Raspberry Pi family.

You will need to disable the JIT and the heavy-weight LLVM dependency which comes with that. EVMJIT only supports x86_64. Other than that, cpp-ethereum should "just work" on 32-bit platforms. To disable JIT, you will need to use the following command for the Makefile generation phase:

```
cmake .. -DEVMJIT=Off
```

Building for Windows We support only 64-bit builds and only for the following versions of Windows:

- Windows 7
- Windows 8/8.1
- Windows 10
- Windows Server 2012 R2

It may be possible to get the client working for Windows 32-bit, by disabling EVMJIT and maybe other features too. We might accept pull-requests to add such support, but we will not put any of our own development time into supporting Windows 32-bit builds.

Pre-requisites You will need to install the following dependencies

Software	Notes
Git for Windows	Command-line tool for retrieving source from Github.
CMake	Cross-platform build file generator.
Visual Studio 2015	C++ compiler and dev environment.

Get the source Clone the git repository containing all the source code by executing the following command:

```
git clone --recursive https://github.com/ethereum/cpp-ethereum.git
cd cpp-ethereum
```

Get the external dependencies Execute the CMake script that downloads and unpacks pre-built external libraries needed to build the project:

```
scripts\install_deps.bat
```

Generate Visual Studio project files Then execute the following commands, which will generate a Visual Studio solution file using CMake:

```
mkdir build
cd build
cmake -G "Visual Studio 14 2015 Win64" ..
```

Which should result in the creation of **cpp-ethereum.sln** in that build directory.

NOTE: We only support Visual Studio 2015 as of cpp-ethereum-v.1.3.0.

Double-clicking on that file should result in Visual Studio firing up. We suggest building **RelWithDebugInfo** configuration, but all others work.

Build on the command-line alternatively, you can build the project on the command-line, like so:

cmake --build . --config RelWithDebInfo

Building for OS X

Overview - Here be dragons! It is impossible for us to avoid OS X build breaks because Homebrew is a "rolling release" package manager which means that the ground will forever be moving underneath us unless we add all external dependencies to our Homebrew tap, or add them as git sub-modules. End-user results vary depending on when they are building the project. Building yesterday may have worked for you, but that doesn't guarantee that your friend will have the same result today on their machine. Needless to say, this isn't a happy situation.

If you hit build breaks for OS X please look through the Github issues to see whether the issue you are experiencing has already been reported. If so, please comment on that existing issue. If you don't see anything which looks similar, please create a new issue, detailing your OS X version, cpp-ethereum version, hardware and any other details you think might be relevant. Please add verbose log files via gist.github.com or a similar service.

The cpp-ethereum-development gitter channel is where we hang out, and try to work together to get known issues resolved.

We only support the following OS X versions:
- OS X Mavericks (10.9)
- OS X Yosemite (10.10)
- OS X El Capitan (10.11

)

The cpp-ethereum code base does not build on older OS X versions and this is not something which we will ever support. If you are using an older OS X version, we recommend that you update to the latest release, not just so that you can build cpp-ethereum, but for your own security.

Clone the repository To clone the source code, execute the following command:

```
git clone --recursive https://github.com/ethereum/cpp-ethereum.git
cd cpp-ethereum
```

Pre-requisites and external dependencies Ensure that you have the latest version of xcode installed. This contains the Clang C++ compiler, the xcode IDE and other Apple development tools which are required for building C++ applications on OS X. If you are installing xcode for the first time, or have just installed a new version then you will need to agree to the license before you can do command-line builds:

```
sudo xcodebuild -license accept
```

Our OS X builds require you to install the Homebrew package manager for installing external dependencies. Here's how to uninstall Homebrew, if you ever want to start again from scratch.

We now have a "one button" script which installs all required external dependencies on macOS and on numerous Linux distros. This used to a multi-step manual process:

```
./scripts/install_deps.sh
```

Command-line build From the project root:

```
mkdir build
cd build
cmake ..
make -j4                (or different value, depending on your number of CPU cores)
```

Install your own build you can also use the same Makefile to install your own build globally on your machine: make install this will install binaries into /usr/local/ and /usr/bin/.

Generate xcode project From the project root:

mkdir build_xc cd build_xc cmake -G Xcode ..

This will generate an Xcode project file called cpp-ethereum.xcodeproj, which you can then open with xcode and build/debug/run.

Building for FreeBSD NOTE - Once the packages are in the FreeBSD main ports this guide should be changed to something much simpler

Install the ports manually for some of this steps you must require a root access to modify the ports directory.

```
curl https://raw.githubusercontent.com/enriquefynn/webthree-umbrella-port/master/libjson-rpc-cpp.
```

Now we execute the script with:

```
cd /usr/ports/devel
sh libjson-rpc-cpp.shar
```

This will create the libjson-rpc-cpp port. Now you should do the same for the webthree-umbrella port, we should get the [webthree-umbrella](https://raw.githubusercontent.com/enriquefynn/webthree-umbrella-port/master/webthree-umbrella.shar) file and create the port under "net-p2p" directory.

```
curl https://raw.githubusercontent.com/enriquefynn/webthree-umbrella-port/master/webthree-umbrell
cd /usr/ports/net-p2p
sh webthree-umbrella.shar
```

Build and Install Now you can navigate to the webthree-umbrella directory and install the port:

```
cd /usr/ports/net-p2p/webthree-umbrella
make install clean
```

Building for Android We don't currently have a working Android build, though that is on the roadmap for doublethinkco. Android uses the Linux kernel, but has a different API than the ARM Linux cross-builds, meaning that specific binaries will be required.

ARM Linux distros use the GLIBC runtime library, where Android uses bionic.

Building for iOS We don't currently have a working iOS build, though that is on the roadmap for doublethinkco. iOS is a UNIX-like operating system based on Darwin (BSD) using ARM chips. This is a different API than the ARM Linux cross-builds, meaning that specific binaries will be required.

Building for Raspberry Pi Model A, B+, Zero, 2 and 3 EthEmbedded maintain build scripts for all Raspberry Mi models. They are on Github in the Raspi-Eth-Install repository. It is also possible to cross-build for these platforms.

Building for Odroid XU3/XU4 EthEmbedded maintain build scripts for both of these Odroid models. Support for a broader range of Odroid devices is likely in the future. They are on Github in the OdroidXU3-Eth-Install repository. It is also possible to cross-build for these platforms.

Building for BeagleBone Black EthEmbedded maintain build scripts for BBB on Github in the BBB-Eth-Install repository. It is also possible to cross-build for this platform.

Building for WandBoard EthEmbedded maintain build scripts for the WandBoard on Github in the
WandBoard-Eth-Install repository. It is also possible to cross-build for this platform.

Building for Linux for ARM (cross builds) doublethinkco maintain a Docker-based cross-build infrastructure which is hosted on Github in the cpp-ethereum-cross repository. At the time of writing, these cross-built binaries have been successfully used on the following devices:
- Jolla Phone (Sailfish OS)
- Nexus 5 (Sailfish OS)
- Meizu MX4 Ubuntu Edition (Ubuntu Phone)
- Raspberry Pi Model B+, Rpi2 (Raspbian)
- Odroid XU3 (Ubuntu MATE)
- BeagleBone Black (Debian)
- Wandboard Quad (Debian)
- C.H.I.P. (Debian)

Still TODO:
- Tizen
- Android
- iOS

Installing binaries
The cpp-ethereum development team and the broader Ethereum community publish binary releases in many different forms for a variety of platforms. This aims to be a complete list of those releases.

If you are aware of other third-party packaging efforts, please let us know on the cpp-ethereum gitter channel, and we will add them to this list.

Docker We are hosting latest development snapshots (and in the future also releases) at docker hub. You can run these images as follows:

Preparation Before running the image, you should pull the latest version and prepare the data directories:

```
# get the lastest version from dockerhub (redo for updates).
docker pull ethereum/client-cpp
# create mountable datadirs; blockchain/account data will be stored there
mkdir -p ~/.ethereum ~/.web3
```

These steps need to be done only once. For upgrading to a new version do the `docker pull` ... again.

Execution The simplest version is to run:

```
docker run --rm -it \
    -p 127.0.0.1:8545:8545 \
    -p 0.0.0.0:30303:30303 \
    -v ~/.ethereum:/.ethereum \
    -v ~/.web3:/.web3 \
    -e HOME=/ \
    --user $(id -u):$(id -g) \
    ethereum/client-cpp
```

This will write data to ~/.ethereum and ~/.web3/ on your host and run the client with your user's permissions. For most cases this should be sufficient and the client should behave exactly as if run from a local build.

If you want the rpc port reachable from the network (not recommended, never do this if you have valuable data or private keys on your machine), replace -p 127.0.0.1:8545:8545 by -p 0.0.0.0:8545:8545.

For convenience, you can create the file /usr/local/bin/docker-eth with the following content:

```
#!/usr/bin/env sh
mkdir -p ~/.ethereum ~/.web3
if ! id -nG $(whoami)|grep -qw "docker"; then SUDO='sudo'; else SUDO=''; fi
$SUDO docker run --rm -it \
    -p 127.0.0.1:8545:8545 \
    -p 0.0.0.0:30303:30303 \
    -v ~/.ethereum:/.ethereum \
    -v ~/.web3:/.web3 \
    -e HOME=/ \
```

CHAPTER 3
Ethereum Tools
Acquiring the Virtual Machine

We have made a virtual machine that contains all of the necessary software. The virtual machine is running Ubuntu 14.04 LTS, Pyethereum and Serpent 2.0. Pyethereum is the program that allows for us to interact with the blockchain and test our contracts. We will be using Pyethereum, a Python based ethereum client, but there are also Ethereum implementations in C++ (cpp-ethereum) and Go (go-ethereum). Serpent 2.0 will allow for us to compile our serpent code into the stack-based language that is actually executed on the blockchain.

The virtual machine requires the host to be a 64-bit operating system, and for optimal performance, hardware acceleration should be turned on (VT-d/AMD-V). Normally, this is turned on by default when supported by your processor. Due to the advanced graphics used in the Ubuntu desktop environment, we recommend turning on 3D acceleration. For more information, refer to your virtual machine's documentation.

Installing Pyethereum and Serpent
NOTE: This section is not required if the provided virtual machine is used. We have preinstalled all of the necessary applications to program Ethereum contracts using Pyethereum and Serpent. The newest version of the virtual machine (and this guide) is available at https://mc2-umd.github.io/ethereumlab/. This section goes over installing a native copy of Pyethereum and Serpent on your machine and give a brief overview of what each component does.

This section assumes you are comfortable with the command line and have git installed. If you need assistance getting git installed on your local machine,

First, let's install Pyethereum. In order to install Pyethereum, we _rst need to download it. Go to a directory you don't mind _les being downloaded into, and run the following command:
git clone https://github.com/ethereum/pyethereum This command clones the code currently in the ethereum repository and copies it to your computer. Next, change into the newly downloaded pyethereum directory and execute the following command git branch develop this will change us into the develop branch. This code is usually stable, and we found that it has better compatibility with the more modern versions of Serpent. Please note that later on, this step may not be necessary as the Ethereum codebase becomes more stable, but with the current rapid

development of Ethereum, things are breaking constantly, so it pays to be on the cutting edge.

Finally, we need to install Pyethereum. Run the following command:
python setup.py install --user
This actually installs Pyethereum on our computer. Note that commands may be di_erent if you are on a non-Unix-like platform. We recommend running Ethereum on Unix-like operating systems such as Mac OS X and Linux.

Now, we are going to install serpent. The steps are extremely similar. Go to the directory that you downloaded ethereum into and run the following commands:

git clone https://github.com/ethereum/serpent
cd serpent
git branch develop
python setup.py install --user
Now that Pyethereum and Serpent are installed, we should test that they are working.
Go to the pyethereum/tests directory and run the following command:
python pytest -m test_contracts.py

If the test states that it was successful, then everything is installed correctly and you are ready to continue with this guide!

The Smart-Contract Programming Model
The Underlying Cryptocurrency. We shall make some simplifying assumptions about the security model of the underlying cryptocurrency. Loosely speaking, we assume that the cryptocurrency has a secure and incentive compatible consensus protocol. The underlying cryptocurrency is based around a blockchain, which allows users to post messages and transfer units of a built-in currency. The data in the blockchain is guaranteed to be \valid" according to the prede_ned rules of the system (e.g., there are no double-spends or invalid signatures). All of the data in the blockchain is public, and every user can access a copy of it. No one can be prevented from submitting transactions and getting them included in the blockchain (with at most some small delay). There is global agreement about the contents of the blockchain history, except for the most recent

handful of blocks (if there are \forks" at all, then longer forks are exponentially more unlikely).

We also assume that the built-in currency (ether, in this case) has a consistent monetary value. Users have an incentive to gain more of (or avoid losing) this currency. Anyone with can acquire ether by purchasing it or trading for it. The currency is assumed to be fungible; one unit of ether is exactly as valuable as any other, regardless of the currency's \history". In reality, existing decentralized cryptocurrencies achieves only heuristic security. But we will make these assumptions nevertheless. How to design a provably secure decentralized consensus protocol under rationality assumptions is a topic of future research. Contracts and Addresses. The system keeps track of \ownership" of the currency by associating each unit of currency to an \address". There are two kinds of addresses: one for users, and one for contracts. A user address is a hash of a public key; whoever knows the corresponding private key can spend the money associated to that address. Users can create as many accounts as they want, and the accounts need not be linked to their real identity.

A contract is an instance of a computer program that runs on the blockchain. It consists of program code, a storage _le, and an account balance. Any user can create a contract by posting a transaction to the blockchain. The program code of a contract is _xed when the contract is created, and cannot be changed. The contract's code is executed whenever it receives a message, either from a user or from another contract. While executing its code, the contract may read from or write to its storage _le. A contract can also receive money into its account balance, and send money from its account balance to other contracts or users.

The code of a contract determines how it behaves when it receives messages, under what conditions (and to whom!) it sends money out and how it interacts with other contracts by sending messages to them. This document is especially about how to write code for useful and dependable contracts.

Transactions, Messages And Gas.
A transaction always begins with a message from a user to some recipient address (either another user or a contract). This message must be signed by the user, and can contain data, ether, or both. If the recipient is a contract, then the code of that contract is executed. If that code contains

an instruction to send a message to another contract, then that contract's code is executed next. So, a transaction must contain at least one message, but can trigger several messages before it completes. Messages act a bit like function calls in ordinary programming languages. After a contract _nishes processing a message it receives, it can pass a return value back to the sender.

In some cases, a contract can encounter a \exception" (e.g., because of an invalid in- struction). After an exception, control is also returned to the sender along with a special return code. The state of all contracts, including account balances and storage is reverted to what it was just prior to calling the exception-causing message.

Ethereum uses the concept of \gas" to discourage overconsumption of resources. The user who creates a transaction must spend some of the ether from that account to purchase gas. During the execution of a transaction, every program instruction consumes some amount of gas. If the gas runs out before the transaction reaches an ordinary stopping point, it is treated as an exception: the state is reverted as though the transaction had no e_ect, but the ether used to purchase the gas is not refunded! When one contract sends a message to another, the sender can o_er only a portion of its available gas to the recipient. If the recipient runs out of gas, control returns to the sender, who can use its remaining gas to handle the exception and tidy up.

4 Simulating Contracts with Pyethereum Tester

In order to test our smart contacts, we will be using the Pyethereum Tester. This tool allows for us to test our smart contracts without interacting with the blockchain itself. If we were to test on a real blockchain - even a private one - it would take a lot of time to mine enough blocks to get our contract published on the blockchain and to run commands on it. Therefore, we use the tester. Below is a simple example that we will use to show how to set up a contract.

```
import serpent
from pyethereum import tester, utils, abi

serpent_code = '''
def multiply(a):
        return(a*2)
'''

s = tester.state()
c = s.abi_contract(serpent_code)

o = c.multiply(5)
print(str(o))
```

Now what is this code actually doing? Let's break it down.

import serpent
from pyethereum import tester, utils, abi
This code imports all of the assets we need to run the tester. We need serpent to compile
our contract. From pyethereum, we need tester to run the tests, we need abi to encode
and decode the transactions that are put on the blockchain, and we need utils for a few
minor operations (such as generating public addresses).
serpent_code = '''
def multiply(a):
return(a*2)
'''
This is our actual serpent code. We will discuss Serpent's syntax later in the guide, but this code contains one function, named multiply(). This function will return a value that is double the parameter a. Please note that the code between the triple quotes is the only non-python code in this section.

s = tester.state()
c = s.abi_contract(serpent_code)

Here, we set up the tester. The _rst line sets up the initial state of the tester - a genesis block. This is the initial block of any block chain. Since we are testing on an independent chain, we will need to start it.
The second line calls the abi contract () function. This will compile the code within our serpent code variable and adds the contract to the block chain. At this point, we can now call multiply () function that we wrote.

o = c.multiply(5)
print(str(o))

Now, we can call any function that we wrote in the contract. When we call a function in the contract, the function call returns exactly what would be returned in serpent, just in python. We store what is returned in variable o. In this case, we simply printed out what was returned, though we can process it anyway we choose. In our example, the contract function returns 10, as expected.

In this case, the person sending the command to the contract is not denned. This isn't a problem in this contract, since the data returned is independent of the sender, it is irrelevant.

However, what if we had a contract, as we will later, where a function is dependent on the sender? Simple, add a parameter that sends the private key of the sender's address.

Below is an example:

o = multiply(5, sender=tester.k0)

In this example, we send the data to the same contract, but the sender is de_ned. If we called msg.sender in our contract, it would return the public key of the sender. Note that tester.k0 represents the private key (we'll go into this more in the next section). This is a unique identi_er for the testing user.

Pyethereum provides 10 of these (tester.k0-tester.k9), each an individual \user".
What if we wanted to send ether? No problem!

o = multiply(5, value=1000, sender=tester.k0)

All, we need to do, as seen in the example, is add a value parameter. We send the value in units of wei.
[5, 9]

Public and Private Keys
All cryptocurrencies are based on some form of public key encryption. What does this mean? It means that messages can be encrypted with one key (the private key) and decrypted with the public key. The Pyethereum tester provides us with fake addresses we can use for testing (tester.k0 - tester.k9), each of them representing an individual party in the contract.

However, these are private addresses that we are using to sign transactions. This tells the world that the sender authorized this transaction to exist. Others can con_rm this by using our public key.

Now, let's say we want someone to be able to submit public keys to a contract as a parameter. How do we calculate the public keys from the private tester keys we have? There is a function in pyethereum's utils that allows for us to do this:

public_k1 = utils.privtoaddr(tester.k1)
data = c.transfer(500,public_k1,sender=tester.k0)

We don't want to send our private key to a contract, because then others could sign transactions as us and take all of our ether! The code above uses the utils.privtoaddr(private key) function, which returns the public key associated with private key. We can then send the public key with the transaction, as we do in line two.

Language Reference
There are several di_erent languages used to program smart contracts for Ethereum. If you are familiar with C or Java, Solidity is the most similar language. If you really like Lisp or functional languages, LLL may be the language for you. The Mutant language is most similar to C. We will be using Serpent 2.0 (we will just refer to this as Serpent, since Serpent 1.0 is deprecated) in this reference, which is designed to be very similar to Python.

Even if you are not very familiar with Python, Serpent is very easy to pick up. Note that all code after this point is Serpent, not Python. In order to test it, it must be put in the serpent code variable mentioned previously. Another thing to note is that many, if not all, of the built-in functions you may come across in other documentation for Serpent 1.0 will work in 2.0.

The log() Function

The log() function allows for easy debugging. If X is de_ned as the variable you want output, log(X) will output the contents of the variable. We will use this function several times throughout this document. Here is an example of it in use:

```
def main(a):
log(a)
return(a)
```

This code will output the variable stored in a. Since we passed in a three, it should be a three. Below is the output of the log function:

('LOG', 'c305c901078781c232a2a521c2af7980f8385ee9', [3L], [])

The part that is important to us is the third piece of data stored in the tuple, speci_cally, the [3L]. This tells us that the value in the variable is a three.

Variables

Assigning variables in Serpent is very easy. Simply set the variable equal to whatever you would like the variable to equal.

Here are a few examples:
```
a = 5
b = 10
c = 7
a = b
```

If we printed out the variables a, b and c, we would see 10, 10 and 7, respectively. Special Variables Serpent creates several special variables that reference certain pieces of data or pieces of the blockchain that may be important for your code. We have reproduced the table from the o_cial Serpent 2.0 wiki tutorial (and reworded portions) for your reference below. [8]

Variable	Usage
tx.origin	Stores the address of the address the transaction was sent from.
tx.gasprice	Stores the cost in gas of the current transaction.
tx.gas	Stores the gas remaining in this transaction.
msg.sender	Stores the address of the person sending the information being processed to the contract
msg.value	Stores the amount of ether (measured in wei) that was sent with the message
self	The address of the current contract
self.balance	The current amount of ether that the contract controls
x.balance	Where x is any address. The amount of ether that address holds
block.coinbase	Stores the address of the miner
block.timestamp	Stores the timestamp of the current block
block.prevhash	Stores the hash of the previous block on the blockchain
block.difficulty	Stores the difficulty of the current block
block.number	Stores the numeric identifier of the current block
block.gaslimit	Stores the gas limit of the current block

Wei is the smallest unit of ether (the currency used in ethereum). Any time ether is referenced in a contract, it is in terms of wei. There are several other denominations as seen in the table below [2]:

Denomination	Amount (in ether)
wei	1.0×10^{18}
Kwei	1.0×10^{15}
Mwei	1.0×10^{12}
Gwei	1.0×10^{9}
Szabo	1.0×10^{6}
Finney	1000
Ether	1
Kether	.001
Mether	1.0×10^{-6}
Gether	1.0×10^{-9}
Tether	1.0×10^{-12}

A very easy to use converter is available at http://ether.fund/tool/converter.

Control Flow
In Serpent, we mostly will use if..elif..else statements to control our programs. For example:

```
a = 5
b = 5
c = 5
if a == b:
a = a + 5
b = b - 5
c = 0
return(c)
elif a == c:
c = 5
return(c)
else:
return(0)
```

Tabs are extremely important in Serpent. Anything that is inline with the tabbed section after the if statement will be run if that statement evaluates to true.

Same with the elif and else statements.
This will also apply to functions and loops when we de_ne those later on.

Important to also note is the not modi_er. For example, in the following code:
```
if not a == b:
return(c)
```
The code in the if statement will not be run if a is equal to b. It will only run if they
are di_erent. The not modi_er is very similar to the ! modi_er in Java and most other
languages. [8]

5.4 Loops
Serpent supports while loops, which are used like so:
```
somenum = 10
while somenum > 1:
```

log(somenum)
somenum = somenum − 1

This code will log each number starting at 10, decrementing and outputting until it gets to 1. [6]

5.5 Arrays
Arrays are very simple in serpent. A simple example is below:
```
def main():
arr1 = array(1024)
arr1[0] = 10
arr1[129] = 40
return(arr1[129])
```

This code above simply creates an array of size 1024, assigns 10 to the zero-th index and assigns 40 to index 129. It then returns the value at index 129 in the array [8, 6].

Functions that can be used with Arrays include:

_ slice(arr, items=s, items=e) where arr is an array, s is the start address and e is the end address. This function splits out the portion of the array between s and e, where s <= e. That portion of the array is returned.
_ len(arr) returns the length of the arr array.

Returning arrays is also possible [8]. In order to return an array, append: arr to the end of the array in the return statement. For example:

```
def main():
arr1 = array(10)
arr1[0] = 10
arr1[5] = 40
return(arr1:arr)
```

This will return an array where the values were initialized to zero and address 0 and 5 will be initialized to 10 and 40, respectively [8].

Strings
Serpent uses two di_erent types of strings. The _rst is called short strings. These are treated like a number by Serpent and can be manipulated as

such. Long strings are treated like an array by the serpent and are treated as such. Long strings are very similar to strings in C, for example. As a contract programmer, we must make sure we know which variables are short strings and which variables are long strings since we will need to treat these di_erently. [8]

Short Strings Short strings are very easy to work with since they are just treated as numbers. Let's declare a couple new short strings:

str1 = "string"
str2 = "string"
str3 = "string3"

Very simple to do. Comparing two short strings is also really easy:

return (str1 == str2)
return (str1 == str3)

The _rst return statement will output 1 which symbolizes true while the second statement will output 0 which symbolizes false. [8]

Long Strings Long strings are implemented similarly to how they are in C, where the string is just an array of characters. There are several commands that are used to work with long strings:

_ In order to de_ne a new long string, do the following:

arbitrary_string = text("This is my string")
_ If you would like to change a speci_c character of the string, do the following:
arbitrary_string = text("This is my string")
setch(arbitrary_string, 5, "Y")

In the sketch() function, we are changing the _fth index of the string arbitrary string to 'Y'.

_ If you would like to have the ASCII value of a certain index returned, do the following:

arbitrary_string = text("This is my string")

getch(arbitrary_string, 5)

This will retrieve the ASCII value at the _fth index in arbitrary string.

_ All functions that work on arrays will also work on long strings.[8, 6]

To check for the equality of two strings, it gets a little more di_cult, and requires the getch() method. An example is given below that returns -1 if str1 and str2 are not equal, and 1 if they are.

```
def compare_equals():
str1 = text("String 1")
str2 = text("String 1")
i = 0
while i < len(str1):
if getch(str1,i) != getch(str2,i):
return(-1)
i = i + 1
return(1)
```

Functions

Functions work in Ethereum very similarly to how they work in other languages. You can probably infer how they are used from some of the previous examples. Here is an example with no parameters:

```
def main():
#Some operations
return(0)
```

And here is an example with three parameters:

```
def main(a,b,c):
#Some operations
return(0)
```

De_ning functions is very simple and makes code a lot easier to read and write [8]. But how do we call these functions from within a contract? We must call them using self.function name(params).

Any time we reference a function within the contract, we must call it from self (a reference to the current contract). Note that any function can be called directly by a user.

For example, let's say we have a function A and a function B. If B has the logic that sends ether and A just checks if the ether should be sent, and A calls B to send the ether, an adversary could simply call function B and get the ether without ever going through the check. We can _x this by not putting that type of logic in separate functions.

Special Function Blocks There are three di_erent special function blocks. These are used to declare functions that will always execute before certain other functions. First, there is in it. The in it function will be run once when the contract is created. It is good for declaring variables before they are used in other functions.

Next, there is shared. The shared function is executed before in it and any other functions. This function is good for if we wanted a constant. Then, the constant would be declared before every other function's execution, so the constant would always exist. Finally, there is the any function. The any function is executed before any other function except the in it function [8].

Sending Wei
Contracts not only can have ether (currency) sent to them (via msg.value), but they can also send ether themselves. msg.value holds the amount of wei that was sent with the contract.

In order to send wei to another user, we use the send function. For example, let's say I wanted to send 50 wei to the user's address stored in x, I would use the code below.

send(x, 50)

This would then send 50 wei from this contract's pool of ether (the ether that other users/contracts have sent to it), to the address stored in x. How do we get a user's address? The easiest way is to store it when that user sends a command to the contract. The user's address will be stored in msg.sender. If we save that address in persistent storage, we can access it later when needed [8] (we will go over persistent storage in the next section).

One thing to note is that the send function will send all of the remaining gas in the contract to the destination address, minus 25. If we want to de_ne how much gas to send, we specify it as the _rst parameter. If we wanted to send only 100 gas, we would send the following:

send(100,x, 50)

Persistent Data Structures
Persistent data structures can be declared using the data declaration. This allows for the declaration of arrays and tuples. For example, the following code will declare a two dimen-sional array: data twoDimArray[][]

The next example will declare an array of tuples. The tuples contain two items each -item1 and item2.

data arrayWithTuples[](item1, item2)

These variables will be persistent throughout the contract's execution (In any function called by any user to the same contract instance). Please note that data should not be declared inside of a function, rather should be at the top of the contract before any function dentitions.

Example:
data arrayWithTuples[](item1, item2)
def someFunction1(params):
....
def someFunction2(params):
....

Now, let's say I wanted to access the data in these structures. How would I do that? It's simple, the arrays use standard array syntax and tuples can be accessed using a period and then the name of the value we want to access. Let's say, for example, I wanted to access the item1 value from the arrayWithTuples structure from the second array address, I would do that like so:

x = self.arrayWithTuples[2].item1

And that will put the item1 value stored in the self.arrayWithTuples array into x.

[8] Note that we will need the self-declaration so the contract knows we are referencing the arrayWithTuples structure in this contract.

Self.storage[] Ethereum also supplies a persistent key-value store called self.storage[]. This is mostly used in older contracts and also is used in our examples below for simplicity. Essentially, put the key in the brackets and set it equal to the value you want.

An example is below when I set the value y to the key x.
self.storage[x] = y

Now whenever self.storage[x] is called, it will return y. For simple storage, self.storage[] is useful, but for larger contracts, we recommend the use of data (unless you need a key- value storage, of course). [8, 6] In this guide, we will use self.storage[], but our \How to Program a Safe Smart Contract" guide's example is much more complex and uses data.

Hashing
Serpent allows for hashing using three deferent hash functions - SHA3, SHA-256 and RIPEMD- 160. The function takes the parameters a and s where a is the array of elements to be hashed and s is the size of the array to be hashed. For example, we are going to hash the array [4,5,5,11,1] using SHA-256 and return the value below. [8]

```
def main(a):
bleh = array(5)
bleh[0] = 4
bleh[1] = 5
bleh[2] = 5
bleh[3] = 11
bleh[4] = 1
return(sha256(bleh, items=5))
```
The output is
[929582240283758951822994575315634114380644899939251667335486235435 0599884701L]
The function de_nitions are:

_ x = sha3(a, size=s) for SHA3
_ x = sha256(a, size=s) for SHA-256
_ x = ripemd160(a, size=s) for RIPEMD-160

Please note that any inputs to the hash function can be seen by anyone looking at the block chain. Therefore, when keeping secrets between two parties, the hash values should be computed o_ of the blockchain then only the hash value put on the block chain. When we want to decode the secret in the hash, we should then send the nonce and the text to the blockchain, rehash it, and compare them with the pre-stored hash value. There is more detail about this process in the accompanying

\How To Program A Safe Smart Contract" guide.

Random Number Generation

In order to do random number generation, you must use one of the previous blocks as a seed. Then, use modulus to ensure that the random number is in the necessary range. In the following examples, we will do just this.

In this example, we will the function will take a parameter a. It will generate a number between 0 and a (including zero).

```
def main(a):
raw = block.prevhash
if raw < 0:
raw = 0 - raw
return(raw%a)
```

Note that we must make sure that the raw number is positive. [4] If we wanted the lowest number to be a number other than zero, we must add that number to the random number generated. Now, when we are referencing previous blocks, we need to make sure there are blocks before our current block that we can reference. On the actual ethereum blockchain, this would not be a big deal since once we build one block on the genesis block; we will always have a previous block. When testing, however, we will need to create more blocks. This will also give us more ether if our tester runs out of ether.

The code to mine a block is below:

```
s.mine(n=1,coinbase=tester.a0)
```

Where n refers to the number of blocks to be mined and coin base refers to the tester address that will \do" the mining. Note that this is python code, and the s variable references the current state of the \blockchain". You cannot mine from inside of a Serpent contract. This function must be used after we have create the state [9]

Gas

As we know, Ethereum smart contracts are essentially small programs. As any programmer knows, in_nite loops and ine_cient code can cause problems. The ethereum network is not extremely powerful, as it is only designed to execute small programs. To incentivize e_cient programming, the execution of contracts requires gas. An amount of gas is \burned" for every operation that occurs in the transaction. Since a contract must be funded, this eliminates the ability for an in_nite loop to occur.

When using the tester, we can simply send an arbitrary amount of gas (that is above the amount the contract needs to execute) since it is free. However, when executing contracts on an actual block chain, we need to make sure that we only spend what we need to. The best way to do this in pyethereum.tester is to use the variable s.block.gas used where s is the current state. These stores the gas used thus far in the current block. Since this is the tester, and we are the only ones putting transactions into the block, this only counts the gas used by our transactions.
Let's look at an example:

```
s = tester.state()
print(s.block.gas_used) #Call 1 = 0 gas
c = s.abi_contract(serpent_code)
print(s.block.gas_used) #Call 2 = 3016 gas
o = c.deposit(value=1000, sender=tester.k0)
print(o)
print(s.block.gas_used) #Call 3 = 3879 gas
```

In the example above, we print the amount of gas used three times. At the _rst call, we have not added any transactions to the block chain, so we have not used any gas yet. At the second call, we have added our contract to the block chain, so we have used 3016 gas.

Let's say we wanted to know how much gas the deposit command used. We can subtract the amount of gas used at call 3 from the amount of gas used at call 2 (3879 – 3016 = 863) to show that calling deposit with the given parameters costs 863 gas.

Now that we know the quantity of gas needed to execute the transaction, we need to _gure out how much that will cost. Currently, on the public block chain, gas cost 10 szabo per unit. However, that unit will adjust when ethereum is o_cially released. The total price of the contract will be equal to the gas price multiplied by the gas cost of the transaction.

Note that when a transaction runs out of gas, the execution of the transaction simply rolls back - it's like it never happened. However, gas and any value sent to the contract or miner will not be refunded. [7, 3]

Sending Wei
Contracts not only can have ether (currency) sent to them (via msg.value), but they can also send ether themselves. msg.value holds the amount of wei that was sent with the contract.

In order to send wei to another user or contract, we use the send function. For example, let's say I wanted to send 50 wei to the user's address stored in x, I would use the code below.

send(x, 50)

This would then send 50 wei from this contract's pool of ether (the ether that other users/contracts have sent to it), to the address stored in x.

How do we get a user's address? The easiest way is to store it when that user sends a command to the contract. The user's address will be stored in msg.sender. If we save that address in persistent storage, we can access it later when needed [8].

One thing to note is that the send function will send all of the remaining gas in the contract to the destination address, minus 25. If we want to de_ne how much gas to send, we specify it as the _rst parameter. If we wanted to send only 100 gas, we would send the following:

send(100,x, 50)

Note that if we are not sending it to another contract, but rather just sending it to a user, we should not send any gas, since the user is not a contract, and therefore does not need gas to complete the transaction.

The Call Stack

The maximum call stack in Ethereum is of size 1024. An attacker could call a contract with an already existing call stack. If a send function (or any function) is called while already at the maximum call stack size, it will create the exception, but the execution of the contract will continue. Therefore, they could cause certain portions of the contract to be skipped.

To solve this, put the following code at the beginning of your functions to ensure that an attacker cannot try to skip portions of the contact:

if self.test_callstack() != 1: return(-1)
Then create the function test callstack():
def test_callstack(): return(1)

This will add a function to the call stack. If an attacker tries to break the call stack, it will cause the contract to not execute.

CHAPTER 4
Peer-to-peer (P2P)

Alternatively, peer-to-peer trading enables individual parties to trade with each other directly. Most of the transactions we make day to day are peer-to-peer: buying coffee at a cafe, selling shoes on eBay, or buying cat food on Amazon. Because these are private transactions between people or businesses, each party knows and ultimately chooses with whom they transact. Peer-to-peer trading scales. Orders are transmitted between individual parties and are one and done as opposed to orders on a public exchange with no guarantee to completely _ll. This makes cancels on an order book a regular occurrence, whereas peer-to-peer orders are likely _lled because they are provided to parties that have already expressed interest. Additionally, peer-to-peer supply and demand matching can be solved through lightweight peer discovery as opposed to expensive algorithmic matchmaking regardless of whether on or o_ chain.

Peer-to-peer trading is private. Once two parties have found and chosen to trade with each other, no third parties are required to negotiate. The communication between these parties remains private for the duration of the negotiation, removing the opportunity for other parties to act on order request behavior. Only when the order is submitted to be _lled will it become public knowledge. Peer-to-peer trading is fair. Because orders are created and transmitted directly between two parties, no outside participants can have an advantage. As long as they are working with multiple independent parties, participants can get prices that are comparable to or better than what they would achieve on an exchange. Additionally, those pricing orders can do so aggressively without fear of being taken advantage of by automated, low-latency trading strategies.

The scalability, privacy, and fairness constraints imposed by blockchain order books have necessitated an alternative. Todays Ethereum ecosystem needs an open peer-to-peer solution for asset exchange.

Introducing Swap
Swap is a protocol to facilitate a true peer-to-peer ecosystem for trading tokens on the Ethereum blockchain. The following is an extensible speci_cation that supports e_cient counterparty discovery and negotiations. These protocols are intended to become a foundation for the asset trading ecosystem and to accelerate Ethereum ecosystem growth. By publishing this paper and opening for discussion, we seek comments from ecosystem stakeholders with the aim to produce high-quality protocols to enable a wide variety of real-world applications.

Peer Protocol
With only a few messages passed between counterparties, trades can be negotiated quickly, fairly, and privately. For the purposes of this document, a Maker is the party that provides an order, and a Taker is the party that _lls it. Because each party is a peer, any party can assume the role of Maker or Taker at any time. Tokens in the following speci_cation are ERC20 compliant and any token that implements the standard can be traded using this protocol.

The core protocol is sequenced in the following diagram. The Maker and Taker perform trade negotiation o_-chain. The Contract below is an Ethereum smart contract, which the Taker calls when ready to _ll an order on the blockchain.

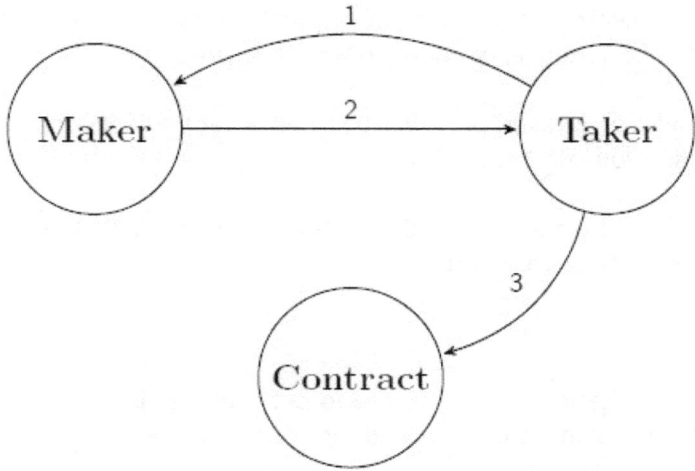

Figure 1: Request, provide, and fill an Order

1. Taker calls getOrder on the Maker.
2. Maker replies with an order.
3. Taker calls fillOrder(order) on the Contract.

Order API

The following APIs are transport-agnostic remote procedure calls (RPC) used to communicate among peers and services. Examples use token tickers instead of addresses, but the actual calls require addresses of ERC20 compliant tokens. The call signatures below are for discussion purposes as further technical details are to be published in a separate document.

The Order API is o_-chain and speci_es asynchronous calls made between counterparties during trade negotiation. An implementor may choose to serve a request-provide cycle as a synchronous request-response. Because an order is signed by the Maker, the Taker is able to later submit it to the smart contract to be _lled.

getOrder(makerAmount, makerToken, takerToken, takerAddress)

Called by a Taker on a Maker, requesting an order to trade tokens.

Example: \I want to buy 10 GNO using BAT."
getOrder(10, GNO, BAT, <takerAddress>)
provideOrder(makerAddress, makerAmount, makerToken, takerAddress, takerAmount, takerToken, expiration, nonce, signature)

Called by a Maker on a Taker, providing a signed order for execution.
Example: \I'll sell you 10 GNO for 5 BAT."

provideOrder(<makerAddress>, 10, GNO, <takerAddress>, 5, BAT, <expiration>, <nonce>, <signature>)

Quote API
Quotes are for indicating price information between parties and are not executable. Quotes can be later turned into orders if the conditions are met for both counterparties.

getQuote(makerAmount, makerToken, takerTokens)
Called by a Taker on a Maker, requesting a quote in speci_c tokens.
Example: \How much would it cost to buy 10 GNO using BAT?"
getQuote(10, GNO, [BAT])
provideQuote(makerAmount, makerToken, takerAmounts)
Called by a Taker on a Maker, providing quotes in Taker tokens.
Example: \It will cost you 5 BAT for 10 G

Indexer Protocol
An Indexer is an o_-chain service that aggregates and matches peers based on their intent to trade: whether prospective Makers and Takers wish to buy or sell tokens. Indexers are o_-chain services that aggregate this intent to trade and help match peers based on intent to buy or sell speci_c tokens. Many prospective Makers can signal intent to trade, and when a Taker asks the Indexer to _nd suitable counterparties, there may be multiple results. Once the Taker has found a Maker with whom they would like to trade, they proceed to negotiate using the Peer Protocol above. Once agreement is reached between a Maker and Taker, the order is _lled on the smart contract.

The interactions between a Maker, Taker, and Indexer are illustrated in the following diagram. The Maker, Taker, and Indexer all operate away from the blockchain and communicate by any preferred messaging medium.

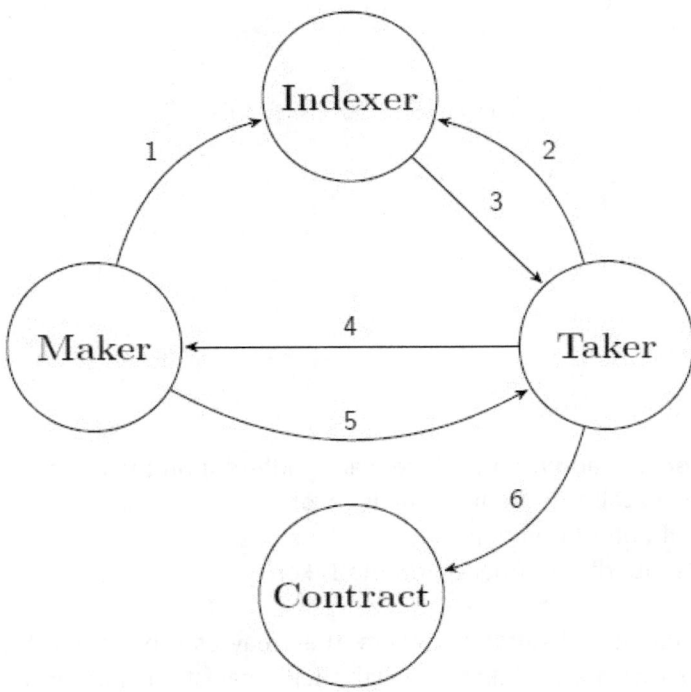

Figure 2: Find a counterparty and make a trade

1. Maker calls addIntent on the Indexer.
2. Taker calls findIntent on the Indexer.
3. Indexer calls foundIntent(maker) on the Taker.
4. Taker calls getOrder on the Maker.
5. Maker replies with an order.
6. Taker calls fillOrder(order) on the Contract.

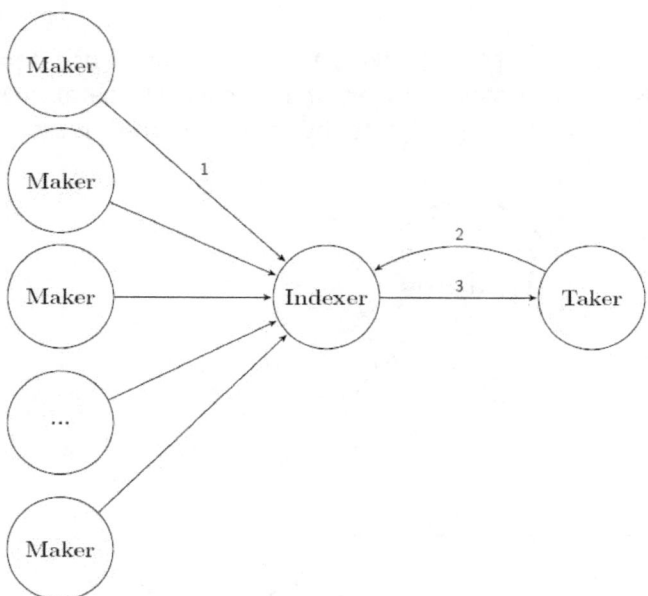

Figure 3: Makers call addIntent, a Taker calls _ndIntent on the Indexer
1. Several Makers call addIntent on the Indexer.
2. Taker calls findIntent on the Indexer.
3. Indexer calls foundIntent(maker) on the Taker.

Once a Taker has found suitable Makers, they may use the Order API to request orders from each Maker to weigh them against each other. If the Taker has decided to _ll a given order, they will make a _llOrder call on the smart contract.

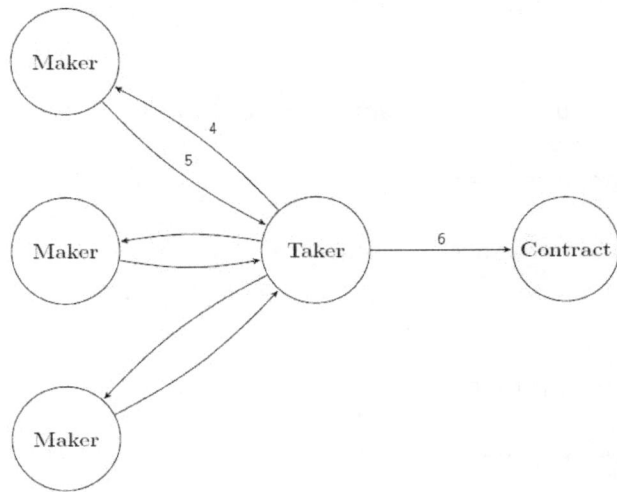

Figure 4: Taker calls getOrder on Makers, Taker calls fillOrder on Contract

4. Taker calls getOrder on several Makers.
5. Several Makers reply with orders.
6. Taker selects an order and calls fillOrder(order) on the Contract.

3.1) Indexer API

The Indexer API manages intent to trade, which is signaled between peers. The following
calls are made between peers and an Indexer.

addIntent(makerToken, takerTokens)

Add an intent to buy or sell some amount of token. Example:

\I want to trade GNO for BAT."
addIntent(GNO, [BAT])
removeIntent(makerToken, takerTokens)

Remove intent to trade tokens.

Example:

\I am no longer interested in trading GNO for BAT."
removeIntent(GNO, [BAT])
getIntent(makerAddress)

List active intent associated with an address.

Example:
\List the tokens that [makerAddress] wants to trade."
getIntent(<makerAddress>)
_ndIntent(makerToken, takerToken)

Find someone willing to trade speci_c tokens.

Example:

\Find someone trading GNO for BAT."
findIntent(GNO, BAT)
foundIntent(makerAddress, intentList)

The Indexer found someone with intent to trade.

Example:

\Found someone selling 10 GNO for BAT."
foundIntent(<makerAddress>, [fmakerAmount: 10, makerToken: GNO, takerTokens: [BAT]g) 9

Oracle Protocol

An Oracle is an o_-chain service that provides pricing information to Makers and Takers. When pricing an order prior to delivering it to a Taker, a Maker may ask the Oracle for what it considers a fair price suggestion? Likewise, having received an order, a Taker may ask the Oracle to check the price on the order to verify that it's fair. The Oracle provides this pricing information to help both the Maker and the Taker make more educated pricing decisions and to smooth the process of trade negotiation.

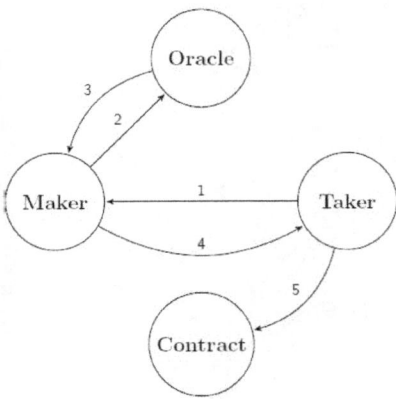

Figure 5: Maker querying Oracle before providing order

1. Taker calls getOrder on the Maker.
2. Maker calls getPrice on the Oracle.
3. Oracle returns a price to the Maker.
4. After analyzing price information, Maker provides an order.
5. Taker calls fillOrder(order) on the Contract.

A very similar interaction happens between Taker and Oracle when the Taker receives an order.

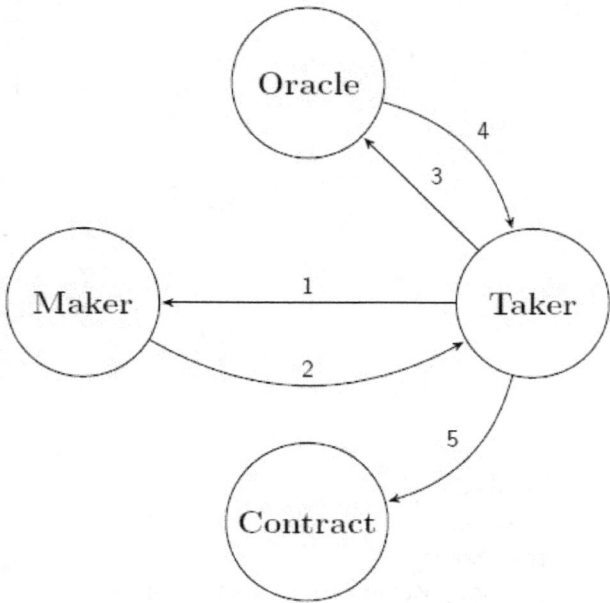

Figure 6: Taker querying Oracle before filling order

1. Taker calls getOrder on the Maker.
2. Maker replies with an order.
3. Taker calls getPrice on the Oracle.
4. Oracle returns a price to the Taker.
5. After analyzing price information, Taker calls fillOrder(order) on the Contract.

Oracle API
The Oracle API is used by Makers and Takers to determine order prices. Prices are suggestions and are not executable.

getPrice(makerToken, takerToken)

Called by a Taker or a Maker on an Oracle to get a price.

Example:

\What is the current price of GNO for BAT?"

getPrice(GNO, BAT)
providePrice(makerToken, takerToken, price)

Called by an Oracle on a Maker or Taker to give a price.

Example:

\The current price of GNO for BAT is 0.5."
providePrice(GNO, BAT, 0.5)

Smart Contract
An Ethereum smart contract to _ll or cancel orders.

_llOrder(makerAddress, makerAmount, makerToken, takerAddress, takerAmount, takerToken, expiration, nonce, signature)

An atomic swap of tokens called by a Taker.

The contract ensures that the message sender matches taker and ensures that the time indicated in expiration has not passed. To _ll orders, peers must have already called approve on the speci_ed tokens to allow the contract to withdraw at least the speci_ed amounts. For token transfers, the contract calls transferFrom on the respective tokens. At the successful completion of this function a Filled event is broadcast to the blockchain.

Example:

\I want to _ll this order of 5 GNO for 10 BAT."
fillOrder([maker], 5, GNO, [taker], 10, BAT, [expiration], [signature])
cancelOrder(makerAddress, makerAmount, makerToken, takerAddress, takerAmount, takerToken, expiration, nonce, signature)

A cancellation of an order that has already been communicated to a Taker but not yet _lled.
Called by the Maker of the order.

Marks the order as already having been _lled on the contract so a subsequent attempt to _ll the order will fail. At the successful completion of this function a Canceled event is broadcast to the blockchain.

Example:

\I want to cancel this order of 5 GNO for 10 BAT."
cancelOrder([maker], 5, GNO, [taker], 10, BAT, [expiration], [signature])

Ether Orders
The smart contract supports trading Ether (ETH) for tokens. If the order includes a null takerToken address (0x0) the smart contract will check the value of Ether that was sent with the function call and transfer that on behalf of the Taker to the Maker.

CHAPTER 5
A NEXT GENERATION SMART CONTRACT & DECENTRALIZED APPLICATION PLATFORM

When Satoshi Nakamoto first set the Bitcoin blockchain into motion in January 2009, he was simultaneously introducing two radical and untested concepts. The first is the "bitcoin", a decentralized
peer-to-peer online currency that maintains a value without any backing, intrinsic value or central issuer. So far, the "bitcoin" as a currency unit has taken up the bulk of the public attention, both in terms of the political aspects of a currency without a central bank and its extreme upward and downward volatility in price.

However, there is also another, equally important, part to Satoshi's grand experiment: the concept of a proof of work-based blockchain to allow for public agreement on the order of transactions. Bitcoin as an application can be described as a first-to-file system: if one entity has 50 BTC, and simultaneously sends the same 50 BTC to A and to B, only the transaction that gets confirmed first will process. There is no intrinsic way of determining from two transactions which came earlier, and for decades this stymied the development of decentralized digital currency. Satoshi's blockchain was the first credible decentralized solution. And now, attention is rapidly starting to shift toward this second part of Bitcoin's technology, and how the blockchain concept can be used for more than just money.

Commonly cited applications include using on-blockchain digital assets to represent custom currencies and financial instruments ("colored coins"), the ownership of an underlying physical device ("smart property"), non-fungible assets such as domain names ("Namecoin") as well as more advanced applications such as decentralized exchange, financial derivatives, peer-to-peer gambling and on-blockchain identity and reputation systems. Another important area of inquiry is "smart contracts" - systems which automatically move digital assets according to arbitrary pre-specified rules. For example, one might have a treasury contract of the form "A can withdraw up to X currency units per day, B can withdraw up to Y per day, A and B together can withdraw anything, and A can shut off B's ability to withdraw". The logical extension of this is decentralized autonomous organizations (DAOs) - long-term smart contracts that contain the assets and encode the bylaws of an entire organization. What Ethereum intends to provide is a blockchain with a built-in fully fledged Turing-complete programming language that can be used to create "contracts" that can be used to encode arbitrary state transition functions, allowing users to create any of the systems described above, as well as many others that we have not yet imagined, simply by writing up the logic in a few lines of code.

History
The concept of decentralized digital currency, as well as alternative applications like property registries, has been around for decades. The anonymous e-cash protocols of the 1980s and the 1990s, mostly reliant on a cryptographic primitive known as Chaumian blinding, provided a currency with a high degree of privacy, but the protocols largely failed to gain traction because of their reliance on a centralized intermediary. In 1998, Wei Dai's b-money became the first proposal to introduce the idea of creating money through solving computational puzzles as well as decentralized consensus, but the proposal was scant on details as to how decentralized consensus could actually be implemented. In 2005, Hal Finney introduced a concept of "reusable proofs of work", a system which uses ideas from b-money together with Adam Back's computationally

difficult Hashcash puzzles to create a concept for a cryptocurrency, but once again fell short of the ideal by relying on trusted computing as a backend.

Because currency is a first-to-file application, where the order of transactions is often of critical importance, decentralized currencies require a solution to decentralized consensus. The main roadblock that all pre-Bitcoin currency protocols faced is the fact that, while there had been plenty of research on creating secure Byzantine-fault-tolerant multiparty consensus systems for many years, all of the protocols described were solving only half of the problem. The protocols assumed that all participants in the system were known, and produced security margins of the form "if N parties participate, then the system can tolerate up to N/4 malicious actors". The problem is, however, that in an anonymous setting such security margins are vulnerable to sybil attacks, where a single attacker creates thousands of simulated nodes on a server or botnet and uses these nodes to unilaterally secure a majority share.

The innovation provided by Satoshi is the idea of combining a very simple decentralized consensus protocol, based on nodes combining transactions into a "block" every ten minutes creating an ever-growing blockchain, with proof of work as a mechanism through which nodes gain the right to participate in the system. While nodes with a large amount of computational power do have proportionately greater influence, coming up with more computational power than the entire network combined is much harder than simulating a million nodes. Despite the Bitcoin blockchain model's crudeness and simplicity, it has proven to be good enough, and would over the next five years becomethe bedrock of over two hundred currencies and protocols around the world.

Bitcoin As A State Transition System

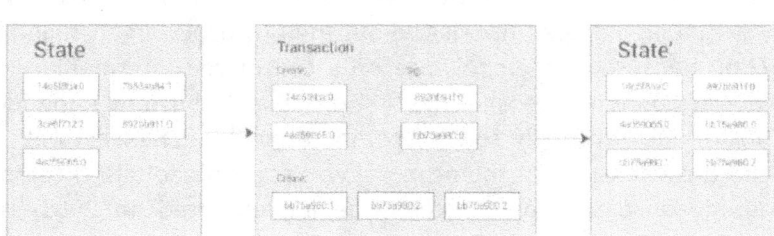

From a technical standpoint, the Bitcoin ledger can be thought of as a state transition system, where there is a "state" consisting of the ownership status of all existing bitcoins and a "state transition function" that takes a state and a transaction and outputs a new state which is the result.

In a standard banking system, for example, the state is a balance sheet, a transaction is a request to move $X from A to B, and the state transition function reduces the value in A's account by $X and increases the value in B's account by $X. If A's account has less than $X in the first place, the state transition function returns an error. Hence, one can formally define:
APPLY(S,TX) >S' or ERROR
In the banking system defined above:

APPLY({ Alice: $50, Bob: $50 },"send $20 from Alice to Bob") = { Alice: $30, Bob: $70 }

But:

APPLY({ Alice: $50, Bob: $50 },"send $70 from Alice to Bob") = ERROR

The "state" in Bitcoin is the collection of all coins (technically, "unspent transaction outputs" or UTXO) that have been minted and not yet spent, with each UTXO having a denomination and an owner (defined by a 20-byte address which is essentially a cryptographic public key[1]). A transaction contains one or more inputs, with each input containing a reference to an existing UTXO and a cryptographic signature produced by the private key associated with the owner's address, and one or more outputs, with each output containing a new UTXO to be added to the state.

The state transition function APPLY(S,TX) >
S' can be defined roughly as follows:

    1. For each input in TX:

        i. If the referenced UTXO is not in S, return an error.
        ii. If the provided signature does not match the owner of the UTXO, return an error.

2. If the sum of the denominations of all input UTXO is less than the sum of the denominations of all output UTXO, return an error.

3. Return S with all input UTXO removed and all output UTXO added.

The first half of the first step prevents transaction senders from spending coins that do not exist, the second half of the first step prevents transaction senders from spending other people's coins, and the second step enforces conservation of value.

In order to use this for payment, the protocol is as follows. Suppose Alice wants to send 11.7 BTC to Bob. First, Alice will look for a set of available UTXO that she owns that totals up to at least 11.7 BTC.

Realistically, Alice will not be able to get exactly 11.7 BTC; say that the smallest she can get is 6+4+2=12. She then creates a transaction with those three inputs and two outputs.

The first output will be 11.7 BTC with Bob's address as its owner, and the second output will be the remaining 0.3 BTC "change", with the owner being Alice herself.

Mining

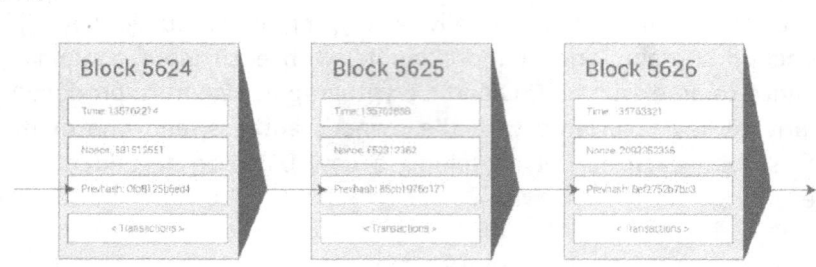

If we had access to a trustworthy centralized service, this system would be trivial to implement; it could simply be coded exactly as described. However, with Bitcoin we are trying to build a decentralized currency system, so we will need to combine the state transition system with a consensus system in order to ensure that everyone agrees on the order of transactions.

Bitcoin's decentralized consensus process requires nodes in the network to continuously attempt to produce packages of transactions called "blocks". The network is intended to produce roughly one block every ten minutes, with each block containing a timestamp, a nonce, a reference to (ie. hash of) the previous block and a list of all of the transactions that have taken place since the previous block. Over time, this creates a persistent, ever-growing, "blockchain" that constantly updates to represent the latest state of the Bitcoin ledger.

The algorithm for checking if a block is valid, expressed in this paradigm, is as follows:

> 1. Check if the previous block referenced by the block exists and is valid
>
> 2. Check that the timestamp of the block is greater than that of the previous block[2] and less than 2 hours into the future.
>
> 3. Check that the proof of work on the block is valid.
>
> 4. Let S[0] be the state at the end of the previous block.
>
> 5. Suppose TX is the block's transaction list with n transactions. For all i in 0...n-1, setS[i+1] = APPLY(S[i],TX[i]) If any application returns an error, exit and return false.
>
> 6. Return true, and register S[n] as the state at the end of this block.

Essentially, each transaction in the block must provide a state transition that is valid. Note that the state is not encoded in the block in any way; it is purely an abstraction to be remembered by the validating node and can only be (securely) computed for any block by starting from the genesis state and sequentially applying every transaction in every block. Additionally, note that the order in which the miner includes transactions into the block matters; if there are two transactions A and B in a block such that B spends a UTXO created by A, then the block will be valid if A comes before B but not otherwise.

The interesting part of the block validation algorithm is the concept of "proof of work": the condition is that the SHA256 hash of every block, treated as a 256-bit number, must be less than a dynamically adjusted target, which as of the time of this writing is approximately 2190. The purpose of this is to make block creation computationally "hard", thereby preventing sybil attackers from remaking the entire blockchain in their favor.
Because SHA256 is designed to be a completely unpredictable pseudorandom function, the only way to create a valid block is simply trial and error, repeatedly incrementing the nonce and seeing if the new hash matches. At the current target of 2192, this means an average of 264 tries; in general, the target is recalibrated by the network every 2016 blocks so that on average a new block is produced by some node in the network every ten minutes. In order to compensate miners for this computational work, the miner of every block is entitled to include a transaction giving them 25 BTC out of nowhere. Additionally, if any transaction has a higher total denomination in its inputs than in its outputs, the difference also goes to the miner as a "transaction fee". Incidentally, this is also the only mechanism by which BTC are issued; the genesis state contained no coins at all.

In order to better understand the purpose of mining, let us examine what happens in the event of a malicious attacker. Since Bitcoin's underlying cryptography is known to be secure, the attacker will target the one part of the Bitcoin system that is not protected by cryptography directly: the order of transactions.

The attacker's strategy is simple:

> 1. Send 100 BTC to a merchant in exchange for some product (preferably a rapid-delivery digital good)
> 2. Wait for the delivery of the product
> 3. Produce another transaction sending the same 100 BTC to himself
> 4. Try to convince the network that his transaction to himself was the one that came first.

Once step (1) has taken place, after a few minutes some miner will include the transaction in a block, say block number 270000. After about one hour, five more blocks will have been added to the chain after that block, with each of those blocks indirectly pointing to the transaction and thus "confirming" it. At this point, the merchant will accept the payment as finalized and deliver the product; since we are assuming this is a digital good, delivery is instant.

Now, the attacker creates another transaction sending the 100 BTC to himself. If the attacker simply releases it into the wild, the transaction will not be processed; miners will attempt to run APPLY(S,TX) and notice that TX consumes a UTXO which is no longer in the state. So instead, the attacker creates a "fork" of the blockchain, starting by mining another version of block 270000 pointing to the same block 269999 as a parent but with the new transaction in place of the old one. Because the block data is different, this requires redoing the proof of work.

Furthermore, the attacker's new version of block 270000 has a different hash, so the original blocks 270001 to 270005 do not "point" to it; thus, the original chain and the attacker's new chain are completely separate. The rule is that in a fork the longest blockchain (ie. the one backed by the largest quantity of proof of work) is taken to be the truth, and so legitimate miners will work on the 270005 chain while the attacker alone is working on the 270000 chain.

In order for the attacker to make his blockchain the longest, he would need to have more computational power than the rest of the network combined in order to catch up (hence, "51% attack").

Merkle Trees
Left: it suffices to present only a small number of nodes in a Merkle tree to give a proof of the validity of a branch. Right: any attempt to change any part of the Merkle tree will eventually lead to an inconsistency somewhere up the chain.

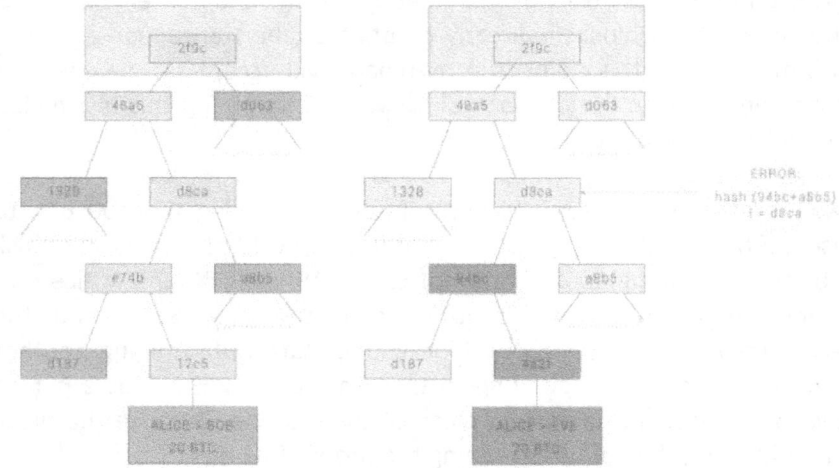

An important scalability feature of Bitcoin is that the block is stored in a multi-level data structure. The "hash" of a block is actually only the hash of the block header, a roughly 200-byte piece of data that contains the timestamp, nonce, previous block hash and the root hash of a data structure called the Merkle tree storing all transactions in the block. A Merkle tree is a type of binary tree, composed of a set of nodes with a large number of leaf nodes at the bottom of the tree containing the underlying data, a set of intermediate nodes where each node is the hash of its two children, and finally a single root node, also formed from the hash of its two children, representing the "top" of the tree. The purpose of the Merkle tree is to allow the data in a block to be delivered piecemeal: a node can download only the header of a block from one source, the small part of the tree relevant to them from another source, and still be assured that all of the data is correct. The reason why this works is that hashes propagate upward: if a malicious user attempts to swap in a fake transaction into the bottom of a Merkle tree, this change will cause a change in the node above, and then a change in the node above that, finally changing the root of the tree and therefore the hash of the block, causing the protocol to register it as a
completely different block (almost certainly with an invalid proof of work).

The Merkle tree protocol is arguably essential to long-term sustainability.

A "full node" in the Bitcoin network, one that stores and processes the entirety of every block, takes up about 15 GB of disk space in the Bitcoin network as of April 2014, and is growing by over a gigabyte per month.

Currently, this is viable for some desktop computers and not phones, and later on in the future only businesses and hobbyists will be able to participate. A protocol known as "simplified payment verification" (SPV) allows for another class of nodes to exist, called "light nodes", which download the block headers, verify the proof of work on the block headers, and then download only the "branches" associated with transactions that are relevant to them. This allows light nodes to determine with a strong guarantee of security what the status of any Bitcoin transaction, and their current balance, is while downloading only a very small portion of the entire blockchain.

Alternative Blockchain Applications
The idea of taking the underlying blockchain idea and applying it to other concepts also has a long history. In 2005, Nick Szabo came out with the concept of "secure property titles with owner authority", a document describing how "new advances in replicated database technology" will allow for a blockchain-based system for storing a registry of who owns what land, creating an elaborate framework including concepts such as homesteading, adverse possession and Georgian land tax. However, there was unfortunately no effective replicated database system available at the time, and so the protocol was never implemented in practice.

After 2009, however, once Bitcoin's decentralized consensus was developed a number of alternative
applications rapidly began to emerge:

- **Namecoin** - created in 2010, Namecoin is best described as a decentralized name registration database. In decentralized protocols like Tor, Bitcoin and BitMessage, there needs to be some way of identifying accounts so that other people can interact with them, but in all existing solutions the only kind of identifier available is a pseudorandom hash like1LW79wp5ZBqaHW1jL5TCiBCrhQYtHagUWy. Ideally, one would like to be able to have an account with a name like "george".

However, the problem is that if one person can create an account named "george" then someone else can use the same process to register "george" for themselves as well and impersonate them. The only solution is a first-to-file paradigm, where the first registrant succeeds and the second fails - a problem perfectly suited for the Bitcoin consensus protocol. Namecoin is the oldest, and most successful, implementation of a name registration system using such an idea.

- **Colored coins** - the purpose of colored coins is to serve as a protocol to allow people to create their own digital currencies - or, in the important trivial case of a currency with one unit, digital tokens, on the Bitcoin blockchain. In the colored coins protocol, one "issues" a new currency by publicly assigning a color to a specific Bitcoin UTXO, and the protocol recursively defines the color of other UTXO to be the same as the color of the inputs that the transaction creating them spent (some special rules apply in the case of mixed-color inputs). This allows users to maintain wallets containing only UTXO of a specific color and send them around much like regular bitcoins, backtracking through the blockchain to determine the color of any UTXO that they receive.

- **Metacoins** - the idea behind a metacoin is to have a protocol that lives on top of Bitcoin, using Bitcoin transactions to store metacoin transactions but having a different state transition function, APPLY'. Because the metacoin protocol cannot prevent invalid metacoin transactions from appearing in the Bitcoin blockchain, a rule is added that if APPLY'(S,TX) returns an error, the protocol defaults to APPLY'(S,TX) = S. This provides an easy mechanism for creating an arbitrary cryptocurrency protocol, potentially with advanced features that cannot be implemented inside of Bitcoin itself, but with a very low development cost since the complexities of mining and networking are already handled by the Bitcoin protocol.

Thus, in general, there are two approaches toward building a consensus protocol: building an independent network, and building a protocol on top of Bitcoin. The former approach, while reasonably successful in the case of applications like Namecoin, is difficult to implement; each individual implementation needs to bootstrap an independent blockchain, as well as building and testing all of the necessary state transition and networking code. Additionally, we predict that the set of applications for decentralized consensus technology will follow a power law distribution where the vast majority of applications would be too small to warrant their own blockchain, and we note that there exist large classes of decentralized applications, particularly decentralized autonomous organizations, that need to interact with each other.

The Bitcoin-based approach, on the other hand, has the flaw that it does not inherit the simplified payment verification features of Bitcoin. SPV works for Bitcoin because it can use blockchain depth as a proxy for validity; at some point, once the ancestors of a transaction go far enough back, it is safe to say that they were legitimately part of the state. Blockchain-based meta-protocols, on the other hand, cannot force the blockchain not to include transactions that are not valid within the context of their own protocols. Hence, a fully secure SPV meta-protocol implementation would need to backward scan all the way to the beginning of the Bitcoin blockchain to determine whether or not certain transactions are valid. Currently, all "light" implementations of Bitcoin-based meta-protocols rely on a trusted server to provide the data, arguably a highly suboptimal result especially when one of the primary purposes of a cryptocurrency is to eliminate the need for trust.

Scripting

Even without any extensions, the Bitcoin protocol actually does facilitate a weak version of a concept of "smart contracts". UTXO in Bitcoin can be owned not just by a public key, but also by a more complicated script expressed in a simple stack-based programming language. In this paradigm, a transaction spending that UTXO must provide data that satisfies the script. Indeed, even the basic public key ownership mechanism is implemented via a script: the script takes an elliptic curve signature as input, verifies it against the transaction and the address that owns the UTXO, and returns 1 if the verification is successful and 0 otherwise. Other, more complicated, scripts exist for various additional use cases. For example, one can construct a script that requires signatures from two out of a given three private keys to validate ("multisig"), a setup useful for corporate accounts, secure savings accounts and some merchant escrow situations. Scripts can also be used to pay bounties for solutions to computational problems, and one can even construct a script that says something like "this Bitcoin UTXO is yours if you can provide an SPV proof that you sent a Dogecoin transaction of this denomination to me", essentially allowing decentralized cross-cryptocurrency exchange.

However, the scripting language as implemented in Bitcoin has several important limitations:

- **Lack of Turing-completeness** - that is to say, while there is a large subset of computation that the Bitcoin scripting language supports, it does not nearly support everything. The main category that is missing is loops. This is done to avoid infinite loops during transaction verification; theoretically it is a surmountable obstacle for script programmers, since any loop can be simulated by simply repeating the underlying code many times with an if statement, but it does lead to scripts that are very space-inefficient. For example, implementing an alternative elliptic curve signature algorithm would likely require 256 repeated multiplication rounds all individually included in the code.

- **Value-blindness** - there is no way for a UTXO script to provide fine-grained control over the amount that can be withdrawn. For example, one powerful use case of an oracle contract would be a hedging contract, where A and B put in $1000 worth of BTC and after 30 days the script sends $1000 worth of BTC to A and the rest to B. This would require an oracle to determine the value of 1 BTC in USD, but even then it is a massive improvement in terms of trust and infrastructure requirement over the fully centralized solutions that are available now. However, because UTXO are all-or-nothing, the only way to achieve this is through the very inefficient hack of having many UTXO of varying denominations (eg. one UTXO of 2k for every k up to 30) and having the oracle pick which UTXO to send to A and which to B.

- **Lack of state** - UTXO can either be spent or unspent; there is no opportunity for multi-stage contracts or scripts which keep any other internal state beyond that. This makes it hard to make multi-stage options contracts, decentralized exchange offers or two-stage cryptographic commitment protocols (necessary for secure computational bounties). It also means that UTXO can only be used to build simple, one-off contracts and not more complex "stateful" contracts such as decentralized organizations, and makes meta-protocols difficult to implement. Binary state combined with value-blindness also mean that another important application, withdrawal limits, is impossible.

- **Blockchain-blindness** - UTXO are blind to blockchain data such as the nonce and previous hash. This severely limits applications in gambling, and several other categories, by depriving the scripting language of a potentially valuable source of randomness.

Thus, we see three approaches to building advanced applications on top of cryptocurrency: building a new blockchain, using scripting on top of Bitcoin, and building a meta-protocol on top of Bitcoin. Building a new blockchain allows for unlimited freedom in building a feature set, but at the cost of development time and bootstrapping effort. Using scripting is easy to implement and standardize, but is very limited in its capabilities, and meta-protocols, while easy, suffer from faults in scalability. With Ethereum, we intend to build a generalized framework that can provide the advantages of all three paradigms at the same time.

Ethereum

The intent of Ethereum is to merge together and improve upon the concepts of scripting, altcoins and on-chain meta-protocols, and allow developers to create arbitrary consensus-based applications that have the scalability, standardization, feature-completeness, ease of development and interoperability offered by these different paradigms all at the same time. Ethereum does this by building what is essentially the ultimate abstract foundational layer: a blockchain with a built-in Turing-complete programming language, allowing anyone to write smart contracts and decentralized applications where they can create their own arbitrary rules for ownership, transaction formats and state transition functions. A bare-bones version of Namecoin can be written in two lines of code, and other protocols like currencies and reputation systems can be built in under twenty. Smart contracts, cryptographic "boxes" that contain value and only unlock it if certain conditions are met, can also be built on top of our platform, with vastly more power than that offered by Bitcoin scripting because of the added powers of Turing-completeness, value-awareness, blockchain-awareness and state.

Ethereum Accounts

In Ethereum, the state is made up of objects called "accounts", with each account having a 20-byte address and state transitions being direct transfers of value and information between accounts. An Ethereum account contains four fields:

- The **nonce**, a counter used to make sure each transaction can only be processed once
- The account's current **ether balance**
- The account's **contract code**, if present
- The account's **storage** (empty by default)

"Ether" is the main internal crypto-fuel of Ethereum, and is used to pay transaction fees. In general, there are two types of accounts: externally owned accounts, controlled by private keys, and contract accounts, controlled by their contract code. An externally owned account has no code, and one can send messages from an externally owned account by creating and signing a transaction; in a contract account, every time the contract account receives a message its code activates, allowing it to read and write to internal storage and
send other messages or create contracts in turn.

Messages and Transactions
"Messages" in Ethereum are somewhat similar to "transactions" in Bitcoin, but with three important
differences. First, an Ethereum message can be created either by an external entity or a contract, whereas a
Bitcoin transaction can only be created externally. Second, there is an explicit option for Ethereum messages to contain data. Finally, the recipient of an Ethereum message, if it is a contract account, has the option to return a response; this means that Ethereum messages also encompass the concept of functions. The term "transaction" is used in Ethereum to refer to the signed data package that stores a message to be sent from an externally owned account. Transactions contain the recipient of the message, a signature identifying the sender, the amount of ether and the data to send, as well as two values called STARTGAS and GASPRICE. In order to prevent exponential blowup and infinite loops in code, each transaction is required to set a limit to how many computational steps of code execution it can spawn, including both the initial message and any additional messages that get spawned during execution. STARTGAS is this limit, and GASPRICE is the fee to pay to the miner per computational step. If transaction execution "runs out of gas", all state changes revert - except for the payment of the fees, and if transaction execution halts with some gas remaining then the remaining portion of the fees is refunded to the sender. There is also a separate transaction type, and corresponding message type, for creating a contract; the address of a contract is calculated based on the hash of the account nonce and transaction data.

An important consequence of the message mechanism is the "first class citizen" property of Ethereum – the idea that contracts have equivalent powers to external accounts, including the ability to send message and create other contracts. This allows contracts to simultaneously serve many different roles: for example, one might have a member of a decentralized organization (a contract) be an escrow account (another contract) between an paranoid individual employing custom quantum-proof Lamport signatures (a third contract) and a co-signing entity which itself uses an account with five keys for security (a fourth contract). The strength of the Ethereum platform is that the decentralized organization and the escrow contract do not need to care about what kind of account each party to the contract is.

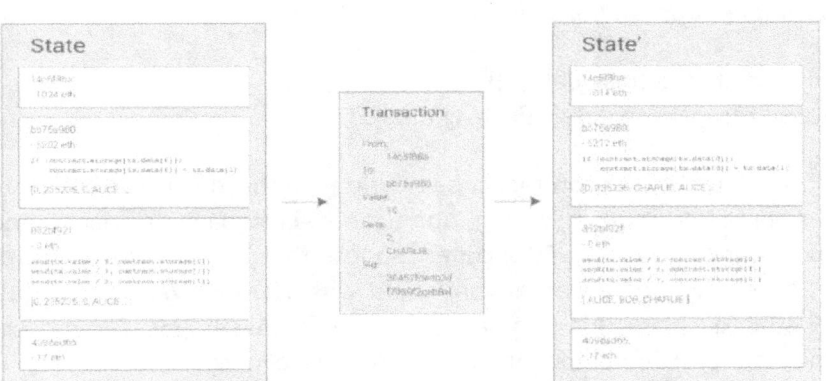

Ethereum State Transition Function

The Ethereum state transition function, APPLY(S,TX) -> S' can be defined as follows:

1. Check if the transaction is well-formed (ie. has the right number of values), the signature is valid, and the nonce matches the nonce in the sender's account. If not, return an error.

2. Calculate the transaction fee as STARTGAS * GASPRICE, and determine the sending address from the signature. Subtract the fee from the sender's account balance and increment the sender's nonce. If there is not enough balance to spend, return an error.

3. Initialize GAS = STARTGAS, and take off a certain quantity of gas per byte to pay for the bytes in the transaction.

4. Transfer the transaction value from the sender's account to the receiving account. If the receiving account does not yet exist, create it. If the receiving account is a contract, run the contract's code either to completion or until the execution runs out of gas.

5. If the value transfer failed because the sender did not have enough money, or the code execution ran out of gas, revert all state changes except the payment of the fees, and add the fees to the miner's account.

6. Otherwise, refund the fees for all remaining gas to the sender, and send the fees paid for gas consumed to the miner.

For example, suppose that the contract's code is:

if !contract.storage[msg.data[0]]:
contract.storage[msg.data[0]] = msg.data[1]

Note that in reality the contract code is written in the low-level EVM code; this example is written in Serpent, our high-level language, for clarity, and can be compiled down to EVM code. Suppose that the contract's storage starts off empty, and a transaction is sent with 10 ether value, 2000 gas, 0.001 ether gasprice, and two data fields: [2, 'CHARLIE'][3]. The process for the state transition function in this case is as follows:

1. Check that the transaction is valid and well formed.

2. Check that the transaction sender has at least 2000 * 0.001 = 2 ether. If it is, then subtract 2 ether from the sender's account.

3. Initialize gas = 2000; assuming the transaction is 170 bytes long and the byte-fee is 5, subtract 850 so that there is 1150 gas left.

4. Subtract 10 more ether from the sender's account, and add it to the contract's account.

5. Run the code. In this case, this is simple: it checks if the contract's storage at index 2 is used, notices that it is not, and so it sets the storage at index 2 to the value CHARLIE. Suppose this takes
187 gas, so the remaining amount of gas is 1150 - 187 = 963

6. Add 963 * 0.001 = 0.963 ether back to the sender's account, and return the resulting state.

If there was no contract at the receiving end of the transaction, then the total transaction fee would simply be equal to the provided GASPRICE multiplied by the length of the transaction in bytes, and the data sent alongside the transaction would be irrelevant. Additionally, note that contract-initiated messages can assign a gas limit to the computation that they spawn, and if the sub-computation runs out of gas it gets reverted only to the point of the message call. Hence, just like transactions, contracts can secure their limited computational resources by setting strict limits on the sub-computations that they spawn.

Code Execution
The code in Ethereum contracts is written in a low-level, stack-based bytecode language, referred to as
"Ethereum virtual machine code" or "EVM code". The code consists of a series of bytes, where each byte
represents an operation. In general, code execution is an infinite loop that consists of repeatedly carrying out the operation at the current program counter (which begins at zero) and then incrementing the program counter by one, until the end of the code is reached or an error or STOP or RETURN instruction is detected. The operations have access to three types of space in which to store data:

- The **stack**, a last-in-first-out container to which 32-byte values can be pushed and popped

- **Memory**, an infinitely expandable byte array

- The contract's long-term **storage**, a key/value store where keys and values are both 32 bytes. Unlike stack and memory, which reset after computation ends, storage persists for the long-term.

The code can also access the value, sender and data of the incoming message, as well as block header data, and the code can also return a byte array of data as an output.

The formal execution model of EVM code is surprisingly simple. While the Ethereum virtual machine is running, its full computational state can be defined by the tuple (block_state, transaction, message, ode, memory, stack, pc, gas), where block_state is the global state containing all accounts and includes balances and storage. Every round of execution, the current instruction is found by taking the pc-th byte of code, and each instruction has its own definition in terms of how it affects the tuple. For example, ADD pops two items off the stack and pushes their sum, reduces gas by 1 and increments pc by 1, and SSTORE pushes the top two items off the stack and inserts the second item into the contract's storage at the index specified by the first item, as well as reducing gas by up to 200 and incrementing pc by 1. Although there are many ways to optimize Ethereum via just-in-time compilation, a basic implementation of Ethereum can be done in a few hundred lines of code.

Blockchain and Mining

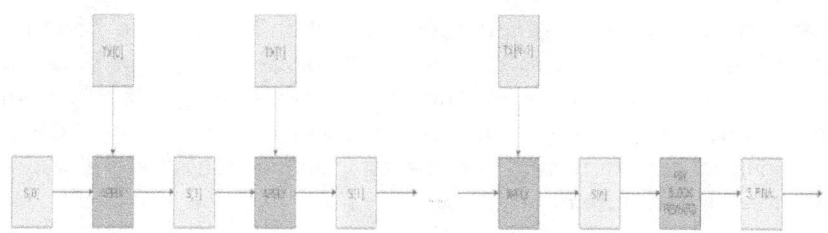

The Ethereum blockchain is in many ways similar to the Bitcoin blockchain, although it does have some differences. The main difference between Ethereum and Bitcoin with regard to the blockchain architecture is that, unlike Bitcoin, Ethereum blocks contain a copy of both the transaction list and the most recent state. Aside from that, two other values, the block number and the difficulty, are also stored in the block.

The block validation algorithm in Ethereum is as follows:

1. Check if the previous block referenced exists and is valid.

2. Check that the timestamp of the block is greater than that of the referenced previous block and less than 15 minutes into the future

3. Check that the block number, difficulty, transaction root, uncle root and gas limit (various low-level Ethereum-specific concepts) are valid.

4. Check that the proof of work on the block is valid.

5. Let S[0] be the STATE_ROOT of the previous block.

6. Let TX be the block's transaction list, with n transactions. For all in in 0...n-1, setS[i+1] = APPLY(S[i],TX[i]).

If any applications returns an error, or if the total gas consumed in the block up until this point exceeds the GASLIMIT, return an error.

7. Let S_FINAL be S[n], but adding the block reward paid to the miner.

8. Check if S_FINAL is the same as the STATE_ROOT. If it is, the block is valid; otherwise, it is not valid.

The approach may seem highly inefficient at first glance, because it needs to store the entire state with each block, but in reality efficiency should be comparable to that of Bitcoin. The reason is that the state is stored in the tree structure, and after every block only a small part of the tree needs to be changed.

Thus, in general, between two adjacent blocks the vast majority of the tree should be the same, and therefore the data can be stored once and referenced twice using pointers (ie. hashes of subtrees). A special kind of tree known as a "Patricia tree" is used to accomplish this, including a modification to the Merkle tree concept that allows for nodes to be inserted and deleted, and not just changed, efficiently. Additionally, because all of the state information is part of the last block, there is no need to store the entire blockchain history - a strategy which, if it could be applied to Bitcoin, can be calculated to provide 5-20x savings in space.

Applications

In general, there are three types of applications on top of Ethereum. The first category is financial applications, providing users with more powerful ways of managing and entering into contracts using their money. This includes sub-currencies, financial derivatives, hedging contracts, savings wallets, wills, and ultimately even some classes of full-scale employment contracts. The second category is semi-financial applications, where money is involved but there is also a heavy non-monetary side to what is being done; a perfect example is self-enforcing bounties for solutions to computational problems. Finally, there are applications such as online voting and decentralized governance that are not financial at all.

Token Systems
On-blockchain token systems have many applications ranging from sub-currencies representing assets such as USD or gold to company stocks, individual tokens representing smart property, secure unforgeable coupons, and even token systems with no ties to conventional value at all, used as point systems for incentivization. Token systems are surprisingly easy to implement in Ethereum. The key point to understand is that all a currency, or token systen, fundamentally is is a database with one operation: subtract X units from A and give X units to B, with the proviso that (i) X had at least X units before the transaction and (2) the transaction is approved by A. All that it takes to implement a token system is to implement this logic into a contract.

The basic code for implementing a token system in Serpent looks as follows:

```
from = msg.sender
to = msg.data[0]
value = msg.data[1]
if contract.storage[from] >= value:
contract.storage[from] = contract.storage[from] value
contract.storage[to] = contract.storage[to] + value
```

This is essentially a literal implementation of the "banking system" state transition function described further above in this document. A few extra lines of code need to be added to provide for the initial step of distributing the currency units in the first place and a few other edge cases, and ideally a function would be added to let other contracts query for the balance of an address. But that's all there is to it. Theoretically, Ethereum-based token systems acting as sub-currencies can potentially include another important feature that on-chain Bitcoin-based meta-currencies lack: the ability to pay transaction fees directly in that currency. The way this would be implemented is that the contract would maintain an ether balance with which it would refund ether used to pay fees to the sender, and it would refill this balance by collecting the internal currency units that it takes in fees and reselling them in a constant running auction. Users would thus need to "activate" their accounts with ether, but once the ether is there it would be reusable because the contract would refund it each time.

Financial derivatives and Stable-Value Currencies
Financial derivatives are the most common application of a "smart contract", and one of the simplest to implement in code. The main challenge in implementing financial contracts is that the majority of them require reference to an external price ticker; for example, a very desirable application is a smart contract that hedges against the volatility of ether (or another cryptocurrency) with respect to the US dollar, but doing this requires the contract to know what the value of ETH/USD is. The simplest way to do this is through a "data feed" contract maintained by a specific party (eg. NASDAQ) designed so that that party has the ability to update the contract as needed, and providing an interface that allows other contracts to send a message to that contract and get back a response that provides the price.

Given that critical ingredient, the hedging contract would look as follows:
1. Wait for party A to input 1000 ether.
2. Wait for party B to input 1000 ether.

3. Record the USD value of 1000 ether, calculated by querying the data feed contract, in storage, say this is $x.

4. After 30 days, allow A or B to "ping" the contract in order to send $x worth of ether (calculated by querying the data feed contract again to get the new price) to A and the rest to B.

Such a contract would have significant potential in crypto-commerce. One of the main problems cited about cryptocurrency is the fact that it's volatile; although many users and merchants may want the security and convenience of dealing with cryptographic assets, they many not wish to face that prospect of losing 23% of the value of their funds in a single day.

Up until now, the most commonly proposed solution has been issuer-backed assets; the idea is that an issuer creates a sub-currency in which they have the right to issue and revoke units, and provide one unit of the currency to anyone who provides them (offline) with one unit of a specified underlying asset (eg. gold, USD). The issuer then promises to provide one unit of the underlying asset to anyone who sends back one unit of the crypto-asset. This mechanism allows any non-cryptographic asset to be "uplifted" into a cryptographic asset, provided that the issuer can be trusted.

In practice, however, issuers are not always trustworthy, and in some cases the banking infrastructure is too weak, or too hostile, for such services to exist. Financial derivatives provide an alternative. Here, instead of a single issuer providing the funds to back up an asset, a decentralized market of speculators, betting that the price of a cryptographic reference asset will go up, plays that role. Unlike issuers, speculators have no option to default on their side of the bargain because the hedging contract holds their funds in escrow. Note that this approach is not fully decentralized, because a trusted source is still needed to provide the price ticker, although arguably even still this is a massive improvement in terms of reducing infrastructure requirements (unlike being an issuer, issuing a price feed requires no licenses and can likely be categorized as free speech) and reducing the potential for fraud.

Identity and Reputation Systems
The earliest alternative cryptocurrency of all, Namecoin, attempted to use a Bitcoin-like blockchain to provide a name registration system, where users can register their names in a public database alongside other data. The major cited use case is for a DNS system, mapping domain names like "bitcoin.org" (or, in Namecoin's case, "bitcoin.bit") to an IP address. Other use cases include email authentication and potentially more advanced reputation systems. Here is the basic contract to provide a Namecoin-like name registration system on Ethereum:

```
if !contract.storage[tx.data[0]]:
    contract.storage[tx.data[0]] = tx.data[1]
```

The contract is very simple; all it is is a database inside the Ethereum network that can be added to, but not modified or removed from. Anyone can register a name with some value, and that registration then sticks forever. A more sophisticated name registration contract will also have a "function clause" llowing other contracts to query it, as well as a mechanism for the "owner" (ie. the first registerer) of a name to change the data or transfer ownership. One can even add reputation and web-of-trust functionality on top.

Decentralized File Storage
Over the past few years, there have emerged a number of popular online file storage startups, the most prominent being Dropbox, seeking to allow users to upload a backup of their hard drive and have the service store the backup and allow the user to access it in exchange for a monthly fee. However, at this point the file storage market is at times relatively inefficient; a cursory look at various existing solutions shows that, particularly at the "uncanny valley" 20-200 GB level at which neither free quotas nor enterprise-level discounts kick in, monthly prices for mainstream file storage costs are such that you are paying for more than the cost of the entire hard drive in a single month. Ethereum contracts can allow for the development of a decentralized file storage ecosystem, where individual users can earn small quantities of money by renting out their own hard drives and unused space can be used to further drive down the costs of file storage.

The key underpinning piece of such a device would be what we have termed the "decentralized Dropbox
contract". This contract works as follows. First, one splits the desired data up into blocks, encrypting each block for privacy, and builds a Merkle tree out of it. One then makes a contract with the rule that, every N blocks, the contract would pick a random index in the Merkle tree (using the previous block hash, accessible from contract code, as a source of randomness), and give X ether to the first entity to supply a transaction with a simplified payment verification-like proof of ownership of the block at that particular index in the tree. When a user wants to re-download their file, they can use a micropayment channel protocol (eg. pay 1 szabo per 32 kilobytes) to recover the file; the most fee-efficient approach is for the payer not to publish the transaction until the end, instead replacing the transaction with a slightly more lucrative one with the same nonce after every 32 kilobytes.

An important feature of the protocol is that, although it may seem like one is trusting many random nodes not to decide to forget the file, one can reduce that risk down to near-zero by splitting the file into many pieces via secret sharing, and watching the contracts to see each piece is still in some node's possession. If a contract is still paying out money, that provides a cryptographic proof that someone out there is still storing the file.

Decentralized Autonomous Organizations
The general concept of a "decentralized organization" is that of a virtual entity that has a certain set of members or shareholders which, perhaps with a 67% majority, have the right to spend the entity's funds and modify its code. The members would collectively decide on how the organization should allocate its funds. Methods for allocating a DAO's funds could range from bounties, salaries to even more exotic mechanisms such as an internal currency to reward work. This essentially replicates the legal trappings of a traditional company or nonprofit but using only cryptographic blockchain technology for enforcement.

So far much of the talk around DAOs has been around the "capitalist" model of a "decentralized autonomous corporation" (DAC) with dividend-receiving shareholders and tradable shares; an alternative, perhaps described as a "decentralized autonomous community", would have all members have an equal share in the decision making and require 67% of existing members to agree to add or remove a member. The requirement that one person can only have one membership would then need to be enforced collectively by the group. A general outline for how to code a DO is as follows. The simplest design is simply a piece of self-modifying code that changes if two thirds of members agree on a change. Although code is theoretically immutable, one can easily get around this and have de-facto mutability by having chunks of the code in separate contracts, and having the address of which contracts to call stored in the modifiable storage. In a simple implementation of such a DAO contract, there would be three transaction types, distinguished by the data provided in the transaction:

- [0,i,K,V] to register a proposal with index i to change the address at storage index K to value V
- [0,i] to register a vote in favor of proposal i

- [2,i] to finalize proposal i if enough votes have been made

The contract would then have clauses for each of these. It would maintain a record of all open storage changes, along with a list of who voted for them. It would also have a list of all members. When any storage change gets to two thirds of members voting for it, a finalizing transaction could execute the change. A more sophisticated skeleton would also have built-in voting ability for features like sending a transaction, adding members and removing members, and may even provide for Liquid Democracy-style vote delegation (ie. anyone can assign someone to vote for them, and assignment is transitive so if A assigns B and B assigns C then C determines A's vote). This design would allow the DO to grow organically as a decentralized community, allowing people to eventually delegate the task of filtering out who is a member to specialists, although unlike in the "current system" specialists can easily pop in and out of existence over time as individual community members change their alignments.

An alternative model is for a decentralized corporation, where any account can have zero or more shares, and two thirds of the shares are required to make a decision. A complete skeleton would involve asset management functionality, the ability to make an offer to buy or sell shares, and the ability to accept offers (preferably with an order-matching mechanism inside the contract). Delegation would also exist Liquid Democracy-style, generalizing the concept of a "board of directors".

In the future, more advanced mechanisms for organizational governance may be implemented; it is at this point that a decentralized organization (DO) can start to be described as a decentralized autonomous organization (DAO). The difference between a DO and a DAO is fuzzy, but the general dividing line is whether the governance is generally carried out via a political-like process or an "automatic" process; a good intuitive test is the "no common language" criterion: can the organization still function if no two members spoke the same language? Clearly, a simple traditional shareholder-style corporation would fail, whereas something like the Bitcoin protocol would be much more likely to succeed. Robin Hanson's futarchy, a mechanism for organizational governance via prediction markets, is a good example of what truly "autonomous" governance might look like.

Note that one should not necessarily assume that all DAOs are superior to all DOs; automation is simply a paradigm that is likely to have have very large benefits in certain particular places and may not be practical in others, and many semi-DAOs are also likely to exist.

Further Applications
1. Savings wallets.
Suppose that Alice wants to keep her funds safe, but is worried that she will lose or someone will hack her private key. She puts ether into a contract with Bob, a bank, as follows:

• Alice alone can withdraw a maximum of 1% of the funds per day.

• Bob alone can withdraw a maximum of 1% of the funds per day, but Alice has the ability to make a transaction with her key shutting off this ability.

• Alice and Bob together can withdraw anything.

Normally, 1% per day is enough for Alice, and if Alice wants to withdraw more she can contact Bob for help. If Alice's key gets hacked, she runs to Bob to move the funds to a new contract. If she loses her key, Bob will get the funds out eventually. If Bob turns out to be malicious, then she can turn off his ability to withdraw.

2. Crop insurance.
One can easily make a financial derivatives contract but using a data feed of the weather instead of any price index. If a farmer in Iowa purchases a derivative that pays out inversely based on the precipitation in Iowa, then if there is a drought, the farmer will automatically receive money and if there is enough rain the farmer will be happy because their crops would do well.

3. A decentralized data feed.
For financial contracts for difference, it may actually be possible to decentralize the data feed via a protocol called "SchellingCoin". SchellingCoin basically works as follows: N parties all put into the system the value of a given datum (eg. the ETH/USD price), the values are sorted, and everyone between the 25th and 75th percentile gets one token as a reward. Everyone has the incentive to provide the answer that everyone else will provide, and the only value that a large number of players can realistically agree on is the obvious default: the

truth. This creates a decentralized protocol that can theoretically provide any number of values, including the ETH/USD price, the temperature in Berlin or even the result of a particular hard computation.

4. Smart multi-signature escrow. Bitcoin allows multisignature transaction contracts where, for example, three out of a given five keys can spend the funds. Ethereum allows for more granularity; for example, four out of five can spend everything, three out of five can spend up to 10% per day, and two out of five can spend up to 0.5% per day. Additionally, Ethereum multisig is asynchronous - two parties can register their signatures on the blockchain at different times and the last signature will automatically send the transaction.

5. Cloud computing. The EVM technology can also be used to create a verifiable computing environment, allowing users to ask others to carry out computations and then optionally ask for proofs that computations at certain randomly selected checkpoints were done correctly. This allows for the creation of a cloud computing market where any user can participate with their desktop, laptop or specialized server, and spot-checking together with security deposits can be used to ensure that the system is trustworthy (ie. nodes cannot profitably cheat). Although such a system may not be suitable for all tasks; tasks that require a high level of inter-process communication, for example, cannot easily be done on a large cloud of nodes. Other tasks, however, are much easier to parallelize; projects like SETI@home, folding@home and genetic algorithms can easily be implemented on top of such a platform.

6. Peer-to-peer gambling. Any number of peer-to-peer gambling protocols, such as Frank Stajano and Richard Clayton's Cyberdice, can be implemented on the Ethereum blockchain. The simplest gambling protocol is actually simply a contract for difference on the next block hash, and more advanced protocols can be built up from there, creating gambling services with near-zero fees that have no ability to cheat.

7. Prediction markets. Provided an oracle or SchellingCoin, prediction markets are also easy to implement, and prediction markets together with SchellingCoin may prove to be the first mainstream application of futarchy as a governance protocol for decentralized organizations.

8. **On-chain decentralized marketplaces**, using the identity and reputation system as a base.

Miscellanea And Concerns

Modified GHOST Implementation

The "Greedy Heaviest Observed Subtree" (GHOST) protocol is an innovation first introduced by Yonatan Sompolinsky and Aviv Zohar in December 2013. The motivation behind GHOST is that blockchains with fast confirmation times currently suffer from reduced security due to a high stale rate - because blocks take a certain time to propagate through the network, if miner A mines a block and then miner B happens to mine another block before miner A's block propagates to B, miner B's block will end up wasted and will not contribute to network security. Furthermore, there is a centralization issue: if miner A is a mining pool with 30% hashpower and B has 10% hashpower, A will have a risk of producing a stale block 70% of the time (since the other 30% of the time A produced the last block and so will get mining data immediately) whereas B will have a risk of producing a stale block 90% of the time. Thus, if the block interval is short enough for the stale rate to be high, A will be substantially more efficient simply by virtue of its size. With these two effects combined, blockchains which produce blocks quickly are very likely to lead to one mining pool having a large enough percentage of the network hashpower to have de facto control over the mining process.

As described by Sompolinsky and Zohar, GHOST solves the first issue of network security loss by including stale blocks in the calculation of which chain is the "longest"; that is to say, not just the parent and further ancestors of a block, but also the stale children of the block's ancestors (in Ethereum jargon, "uncles") are added to the calculation of which block has the largest total proof of work backing it. To solve the second issue of centralization bias, we go beyond the protocol described by Sompolinsky and Zohar, and also allow stales to be registered into the main chain to receive a block reward: a stale block receives 93.75% of its base reward, and the nephew that includes the stale block receives the remaining 6.25%. Transaction fees, however, are not awarded to uncles.

Ethereum implements a simplified version of GHOST which only goes down five levels. Specifically, a stale block can only be included as an uncle by the 2nd to 5th generation child of its parent, and not any block with a more distant relation (eg. 6th generation child of a parent, or 3rd generation child of a grandparent). This was done for several reasons. First, unlimited GHOST would include too many complications into the calculation of which uncles for a given block are valid. Second, unlimited GHOST with compensation as used in Ethereum removes the incentive for a miner to mine on the main chain and not the chain of a public attacker. Finally, calculations show that five-level GHOST with incentivization is over 95% efficient even with a 15s block time, and miners with 25% hashpower show centralization gains of less than 3%.

Fees

Because every transaction published into the blockchain imposes on the network the cost of needing to download and verify it, there is a need for some regulatory mechanism, typically involving transaction fees, to prevent abuse. The default approach, used in Bitcoin, is to have purely voluntary fees, relying on miners to act as the gatekeepers and set dynamic minimums. This approach has been received very favorably in the Bitcoin community particularly because it is "market-based", allowing supply and demand between miners and transaction senders determine the price. The problem with this line of reasoning is, however, that transaction processing is not a market; although it is intuitively attractive to construe transaction processing as a service that the miner is offering to the sender, in reality every transaction that a miner includes will need to be processed by every node in the network, so the vast majority of the cost of transaction processing is borne by third parties and not the miner that is making the decision of whether or not to include it. Hence, tragedy-of-the-commons problems are very likely to occur.

However, as it turns out this flaw in the market-based mechanism, when given a particular inaccurate simplifying assumption, magically cancels itself out. The argument is as follows. Suppose that:

1. A transaction leads to k operations, offering the reward kR to any miner that includes it where R is set by the sender and k and R are (roughly) visible to the miner beforehand.

2. An operation has a processing cost of C to any node (ie. all nodes have equal efficiency)

3. There are N mining nodes, each with exactly equal processing power (ie. 1/N of total)

4. No non-mining full nodes exist.

A miner would be willing to process a transaction if the expected reward is greater than the cost. Thus, the expected reward is kR/N since the miner has a 1/N chance of processing the next block, and the processing cost for the miner is simply kC. Hence, miners will include transactions where kR/N > kC, or R > NC. Note that R is the per-operation fee provided by the sender, and is thus a lower bound on the benefit that the sender derives from the transaction, and NC is the cost to the entire network together of processing an operation.

Hence, miners have the incentive to include only those transactions for which the total utilitarian benefit exceeds the cost.

However, there are several important deviations from those assumptions in reality:

1. The miner does pay a higher cost to process the transaction than the other verifying nodes, since the extra verification time delays block propagation and thus increases the chance the block will become a stale.

2. There are exist non-mining full nodes.

3. The mining power distribution may end up radically in egalitarian in practice.

4. Speculators, political enemies and crazies whose utility function includes causing harm to the network do exist, and they can cleverly set up contracts whose cost is much lower than the cost paid by other verifying nodes.

Point 1 above provides a tendency for the miner to include fewer transactions, and point 2 increases NC; hence, these two effects at least partially cancel each other out. Points 3 and 4 are the major issue; to solve them we simply institute a floating cap: no block can have more operations than BLK_LIMIT_FACTOR times the long-term exponential moving average.

Specifically:
blk.oplimit = floor((blk.parent.oplimit * (EMAFACTOR - 1) + floor(parent.opcount * BLK_LIMIT_FACTOR)) /EMA_FACTOR)BLK_LIMIT_FACTOR and EMA_FACTOR are constants that will be set to 65536 and 1.5 for the time being, but will likely be changed after further analysis.

Computation And Turing-Completeness

An important note is that the Ethereum virtual machine is Turing-complete; this means that EVM code can encode any computation that can be conceivably carried out, including infinite loops. EVM code allows looping in two ways. First, there is a JUMP instruction that allows the program to jump back to a previous spot in the code, and a JUMPI instruction to do conditional jumping, allowing for statements like while x < 27: x = x * 2.

Second, contracts can call other contracts, potentially allowing for looping through recursion. This naturally leads to a problem: can malicious users essentially shut miners and full nodes down by forcing them to enter into an infinite loop? The issue arises because of a problem in computer science known as the halting problem: there is no way to tell, in the general case, whether or not a given program will ever halt. As described in the state transition section, our solution works by requiring a transaction to set a maximum number of computational steps that it is allowed to take, and if execution takes longer computation is reverted but fees are still paid. Messages work in the same way. To show the motivation behind our solution, consider the following examples:

• An attacker creates a contract which runs an infinite loop, and then sends a transaction activating that loop to the miner. The miner will process the transaction, running the infinite loop, and wait for it to run out of gas. Even though the execution runs out of gas and stops halfway through, the transaction is still valid and the miner still claims the fee from the attacker for each computational step.

• An attacker creates a very long infinite loop with the intent of forcing the miner to keep computing for such a long time that by the time computation finishes a few more blocks will have come out and it will not be possible for the miner to include the transaction to claim the fee. However, the attacker will be required to submit a value for STARTGAS limiting the number of computational steps that execution can take, so the miner will know ahead of time that the computation will take an excessively large number of steps.

- An attacker sees a contract with code of some form like send (A,contract.storage[A]); contract.storage[A] = 0, and sends a transaction with just enough gas to run the first step but not the second (ie. making a withdrawal but not letting the balance go down). The contract author does not need to worry about protecting against such attacks, because if execution stops halfway through the changes get reverted.

- A financial contract works by taking the median of nine proprietary data feeds in order to minimize risk. An attacker takes over one of the data feeds, which is designed to be modifiable via the variable-address-call mechanism described in the section on DAOs, and converts it to run an infinite loop, hereby attempting to force any attempts to claim funds from the financial contract to run out of gas. However, the financial contract can set a gas limit on the message to prevent this problem.

The alternative to Turing-completeness is Turing-incompleteness, where JUMP and JUMPI do not exist and only one copy of each contract is allowed to exist in the call stack at any given time. With this system, the fee system described and the uncertainties around the effectiveness of our solution might not be necessary, as the cost of executing a contract would be bounded above by its size. Additionally, Turing-incompleteness is not even that big a limitation; out of all the contract examples we have conceived internally, so far only one required a loop, and even that loop could be removed by making 26 repetitions of a one-line piece of code. Given the serious implications of Turing-completeness, and the limited benefit, why not simply has a Turing-incomplete language? In reality, however, Turing- incompleteness is far from a neat solution to the problem. To see why, consider the following contracts:

C0: call(C1); call(C1);
C1: call(C2); call(C2);
C2: call(C3); call(C3);
...
C49: call(C50); call(C50);
C50: (run one step of a program and record the change in storage)

Now, send a transaction to A. Thus, in 51 transactions, we have a contract that takes up 250 computational steps. Miners could try to detect such logic bombs ahead of time by maintaining a value alongside each contract specifying the maximum number of computational steps that it can take, and calculating this for contracts calling other contracts recursively, but that would require miners to forbid contracts that create other contracts (since the creation and execution of all 50 contracts above could easily be rolled into a single contract). Another problematic point is that the address field of a message is a variable, so in general it may not even be possible to tell which other contracts a given contract will call ahead of time. Hence, all in all, we have a surprising conclusion: Turing-completeness is surprisingly easy to manage, and the lack of Turing-completeness is equally surprisingly difficult to manage unless the exact same controls are in place - but in that case why not just let the protocol be Turing-complete?

Currency And Issuance

The Ethereum network includes its own built-in currency, ether, which serves the dual purpose of providing a primary liquidity layer to allow for efficient exchange between various types of digital assets and, more importantly, of providing a mechanism for paying transaction fees. For convenience and to avoid future argument (see the current mBTC/uBTC/satoshi debate in Bitcoin), the denominations will be pre-labelled:
- 1: wei
- 10^{12}: szabo
- 10^{15}: finney
- 10^{18}: ether

This should be taken as an expanded version of the concept of "dollars" and "cents" or "BTC" and "satoshi". In the near future, we expect "ether" to be used for ordinary transactions, "finney" for microtransactions and "szabo" and "wei" for technical discussions around fees and protocol implementation.

The issuance model will be as follows:

- Ether will be released in a currency sale at the price of 1337-2000 ether per BTC, a mechanism intended to fund the Ethereum organization and pay for development that has been used with success by a number of other cryptographic platforms. Earlier buyers will benefit from larger discounts. The BTC received from the sale will be used entirely to pay salaries and bounties to developers, researchers and projects in the cryptocurrency ecosystem.

• 0.099x the total amount sold will be allocated to early contributors who participated in development before BTC funding or certainty of funding was available, and another 0.099x will be allocated to long-term research projects.

• 0.26x the total amount sold will be allocated to miners per year forever after that point.

Issuance Breakdown
The permanent linear supply growth model reduces the risk of what some see as excessive wealth concentration in Bitcoin, and gives individuals living in present and future eras a fair chance to acquire currency units, while at the same time discouraging depreciation of ether because the "supply growth rate" as a percentage still tends to zero over time. We also theorize that because coins are always lost over time due to carelessness, death, etc, and coin loss can be modeled as a percentage of the total supply per year, that the total currency supply in circulation will in fact eventually stabilize at a value equal to the annual issuance divided by the loss rate (eg. at a loss rate of 1%, once the supply reaches 26X then 0.26X will be mined and 0.26X lost every year, creating an equilibrium).

Group	At launch	After 1 year	After 5 years
Currency units	1.198X	1.458X	2.498X
Purchasers	83.5%	68.6%	40.0%
Early contributor distribution	8.26%	6.79%	3.96%
Long-term endowment	8.26%	6.79%	3.96%
Miners	0%	17.8%	52.0%

Despite the linear currency issuance, just like with Bitcoin over time the supply growth rate nevertheless tends to zero.

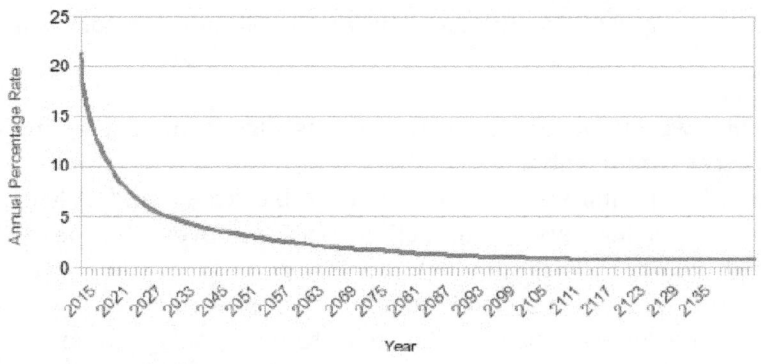

Anticipated Ether Supply Growth Rate

Mining Centralization

The Bitcoin mining algorithm basically works by having miners compute SHA256 on slightly modified versions of the block header millions of times over and over again, until eventually one node comes up with a version whose hash is less than the target (currently around 2190). However, this mining algorithm is vulnerable to two forms of centralization. First, the mining ecosystem has come to be dominated by ASICs (application-specific integrated circuits), computer chips designed for, and therefore thousands of times more efficient at, the specific task of Bitcoin mining. This means that Bitcoin mining is no longer a highly decentralized and egalitarian pursuit, requiring millions of dollars of capital to effectively participate in. Second, most Bitcoin miners do not actually perform block validation locally; instead, they rely on a centralized mining pool to provide the block headers. This problem is arguably worse: as of the time of this writing, the top two mining pools indirectly control roughly 50% of processing power in the Bitcoin network, although this is mitigated by the fact that miners can switch to other mining pools if a pool or coalition attempts a 51% attack.

The current intent at Ethereum is to use a mining algorithm based on randomly generating a unique hash function for every 1000 nonces, using a sufficiently broad range of computation to remove the benefit of specialized hardware. Such a strategy will certainly not reduce the gain of centralization to zero, but it does not need to. Note that each individual user, on their private laptop or desktop, can perform a certain quantity of mining activity almost for free, paying only electricity costs, but after the point of 100% CPU utilization of their computer additional mining will require them to pay for both electricity and hardware. ASIC mining companies need to pay for electricity and hardware starting from the first hash. Hence, if the centralization gain can be kept to below this ratio, (E + H) / E, then even if ASICs are made there will still be room for ordinary miners.

Additionally, we intend to design the mining algorithm so that mining requires access to the entire
blockchain, forcing miners to store the entire blockchain and at least be capable of verifying every transaction. This removes the need for centralized mining pools; although mining pools can still serve the legitimate role of evening out the randomness of reward distribution, this function can be served equally well by peer-to-peer pools with no central control. It additionally helps fight centralization, by increasing the number of full nodes in the network so that the network remains reasonably decentralized even if most ordinary users prefer light clients.

Scalability
One common concern about Ethereum is the issue of scalability. Like Bitcoin, Ethereum suffers from the flaw that every transaction needs to be processed by every node in the network. With Bitcoin, the size of the current blockchain rests at about 20 GB, growing by about 1 MB per hour. If the Bitcoin network were to process Visa's 2000 transactions per second, it would grow by 1 MB per three seconds (1 GB per hour, 8 TB per year). Ethereum is likely to suffer a similar growth pattern, worsened by the fact that there will be many applications on top of the Ethereum blockchain instead of just a currency as is the case with Bitcoin, but

ameliorated by the fact that Ethereum full nodes need to store just the state instead of the entire blockchain history. The problem with such a large blockchain size is centralization risk. If the blockchain size increases to, say, 100 TB, then the likely scenario would be that only a very small number of large businesses would run full nodes, with all regular users using light SPV nodes. In such a situation, there arises the potential concern that the full nodes could band together and all agree to cheat in some profitable fashion (eg. change the block reward, give themselves BTC). Light nodes would have no way of detecting this immediately. Of course, at least one honest full node would likely exist, and after a few hours information about the fraud would trickle out through channels like Reddit, but at that point it would be too late: it would be up to the ordinary users to organize an effort to blacklist the given blocks, a massive and likely infeasible coordination problem on a similar scale as that of pulling off a successful 51% attack. In the case of Bitcoin, this is currently a problem, but there exists a blockchain modification suggested by Peter Todd which will alleviate this issue.

In the near term, Ethereum will use two additional strategies to cope with this problem. First, because of the blockchain-based mining algorithms, at least every miner will be forced to be a full node, creating a lower bound on the number of full nodes. Second and more importantly, however, we will include an intermediate state tree root in the blockchain after processing each transaction. Even if block validation is centralized, as long as one honest verifying node exists, the centralization problem can be circumvented via a verification protocol.

If a miner publishes an invalid block, that block must either be badly formatted, or the state S[n] is incorrect. Since S[0] is known to be correct, there must be some first state S[i] that is incorrect where S[i-1] is correct. The verifying node would provide the index i, along with a "proof of invalidity" consisting of the subset of Patricia tree nodes needing to process APPLY(S[i-1],TX[i]) -> S[i]. Nodes would be able to use those nodes to run that part of the computation, and see that the S[i] generated does not match the S[i] provided.

Another, more sophisticated, attack would involve the malicious miners publishing incomplete blocks, so the full information does not even exist to determine whether or not blocks are valid. The solution to this is a challenge-response protocol: verification nodes issue "challenges" in the form of target transaction indices, and upon receiving a node a light node treats the block as untrusted until another node, whether the miner or another verifier, provides a subset of Patricia nodes as a proof of validity.

Putting It All Together: Decentralized Applications
The contract mechanism described above allows anyone to build what is essentially a command line application run on a virtual machine that is executed by consensus across the entire network, allowing it to modify a globally accessible state as its "hard drive". However, for most people, the command line interface that is the transaction sending mechanism is not sufficiently user-friendly to make decentralization an attractive mainstream alternative.

To this end, a complete "decentralized application" should consist of both low-level business-logic components, whether implemented entirely on Ethereum, using a combination of Ethereum and other systems (eg. a P2P messaging layer, one of which is currently planned to be put into the Ethereum clients) or other systems entirely, and high-level graphical user interface components.

The Ethereum client's design is to serve as a web browser, but include support for a "eth" Javascript API object, which specialized web pages viewed in the client will be able to use to interact with the Ethereum blockchain. From the point of view of the "traditional" web, these web pages are entirely static content, since the blockchain and other decentralized protocols will serve as a complete replacement for the server for the purpose of handling user-initiated requests.

Eventually, decentralized protocols, hopefully themselves in some fashion using Ethereum, may be used to store the web pages themselves.

CHAPTER 6
Transactions
We define an electronic coin as a chain of digital signatures. Each owner transfers the coin to the next by digitally signing a hash of the previous transaction and the public key of the next owner and adding these to the end of the coin. A payee can verify the signatures to verify the chain of ownership.

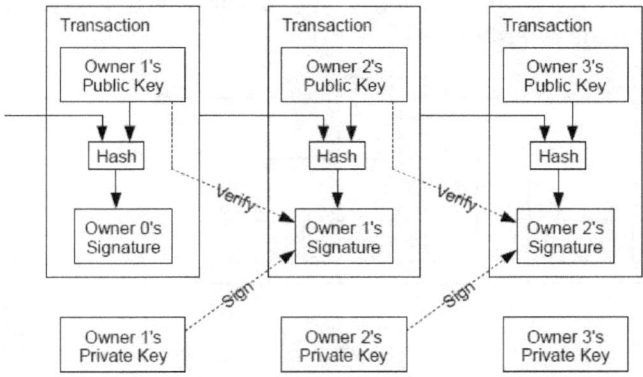

The problem of course is the payee can't verify that one of the owners did not double-spend the coin. A common solution is to introduce a trusted central authority, or mint, that checks every transaction for double spending. After each transaction, the coin must be returned to the mint to issue a new coin, and only coins issued directly from the mint are trusted not to be double-spent.

The problem with this solution is that the fate of the entire money system depends on the company running the mint, with every transaction having to go through them, just like a bank. We need a way for the payee to know that the previous owners did not sign any earlier transactions. For our purposes, the earliest transaction is the one that counts, so we don't care about later attempts to double-spend. The only way to confirm the absence of a transaction is to be aware of all transactions. In the mint based model, the mint was aware of all transactions and decided which arrived first. To accomplish this without a trusted party, transactions must be publicly announced [1], and we need a system for participants to agree on a single history of the order in which they were received. The payee needs proof that at the time of each transaction, the majority of nodes agreed it was the first received.

Timestamp Server
The solution we propose begins with a timestamp server. A timestamp server works by taking a hash of a block of items to be time stamped and widely publishing the hash, such as in a newspaper or Usenet post [2-5]. The timestamp proves that the data must have existed at the time, obviously, in order to get into the hash. Each timestamp includes the

previous timestamp in its hash, forming a chain, with each additional timestamp reinforcing the ones before it.

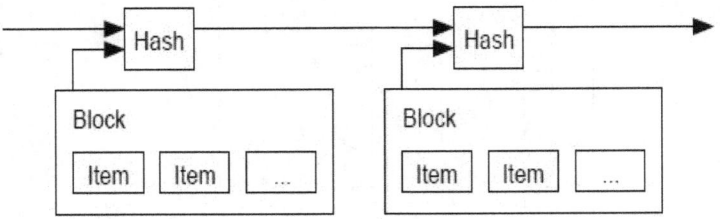

Proof-of-Work

To implement a distributed timestamp server on a peer-to-peer basis, we will need to use a proof-of-work system similar to Adam Back's Hashcash [6], rather than newspaper or Usenet posts. The proof-of-work involves scanning for a value that when hashed, such as with SHA-256, the hash begins with a number of zero bits. The average work required is exponential in the number of zero bits required and can be verified by executing a single hash. For our timestamp network, we implement the proof-of-work by incrementing a nonce in the block until a value is found that gives the block's hash the required zero bits. Once the CPU effort has been expended to make it satisfy the proof-of-work, the block cannot be changed without redoing the work. As later blocks are chained after it, the work to change the block would include redoing all the blocks after it.

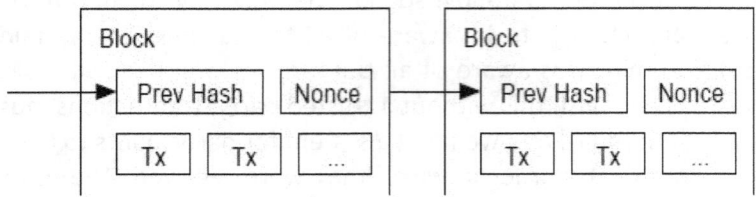

The proof-of-work also solves the problem of determining representation in majority decision making. If the majority were based on one-IP-address-one-vote, it could be subverted by anyone able to allocate many IPs. Proof-of-work is essentially one-CPU-one-vote.

The majority decision is represented by the longest chain, which has the greatest proof-of-work effort invested in it. If a majority of CPU power is controlled by honest nodes, the honest chain will grow the fastest and outpace any competing chains.

To modify a past block, an attacker would have to redo the proof-of-work of the block and all blocks after it and then catch up with and surpass the work of the honest nodes. We will show later that the probability of a slower attacker catching up diminishes exponentially as subsequent blocks are added. To compensate for increasing hardware speed and varying interest in running nodes over time, the proof-of-work difficulty is determined by a moving average targeting an average number of blocks per hour. If they're generated too fast, the difficulty increases.

Network
The steps to run the network are as follows:

1) New transactions are broadcast to all nodes.
2) Each node collects new transactions into a block.
3) Each node works on finding a difficult proof-of-work for its block.
4) When a node finds a proof-of-work, it broadcasts the block to all nodes.
5) Nodes accept the block only if all transactions in it are valid and not already spent.
6) Nodes express their acceptance of the block by working on creating the next block in the chain, using the hash of the accepted block as the previous hash.

Nodes always consider the longest chain to be the correct one and will keep working on extending it. If two nodes broadcast different versions of the next block simultaneously, some nodes may receive one or the other first. In that case, they work on the first one they received, but save the other branch in case it becomes longer. The tie will be broken when the next proof-of-work is found and one branch becomes longer; the nodes that were working on the other branch will then switch to the longer one.

New transaction broadcasts do not necessarily need to reach all nodes. As long as they reach many nodes, they will get into a block before long. Block broadcasts are also tolerant of dropped messages. If a node does not receive a block, it will request it when it receives the next block and realizes it missed one.

Incentive

By convention, the first transaction in a block is a special transaction that starts a new coin owned by the creator of the block. This adds an incentive for nodes to support the network, and provides a way to initially distribute coins into circulation, since there is no central authority to issue them. The steady addition of a constant of amount of new coins is analogous to gold miners expending resources to add gold to circulation. In our case, it is CPU time and electricity that is expended. The incentive can also be funded with transaction fees. If the output value of a transaction is less than its input value, the difference is a transaction fee that is added to the incentive value of the block containing the transaction. Once a predetermined number of coins have entered circulation, the incentive can transition entirely to transaction fees and be completely inflation free. The incentive may help encourage nodes to stay honest. If a greedy attacker is able to assemble more CPU power than all the honest nodes, he would have to choose between using it to defraud people by stealing back his payments, and using it to generate new coins. He ought to find it more profitable to play by the rules, such rules that favors him with more new coins than everyone else combined, than to undermine the system and the validity of his own wealth.

Reclaiming Disk Space

Once the latest transaction in a coin is buried under enough blocks, the spent transactions before
It can be discarded to save disk space. To facilitate this without breaking the block's hash, Transactions are hashed in a Merkle Tree [7][2][5], with only the root included in the block's hash. Old blocks can then be compacted by stubbing off branches of the tree. The interior hashes do not need to be stored.

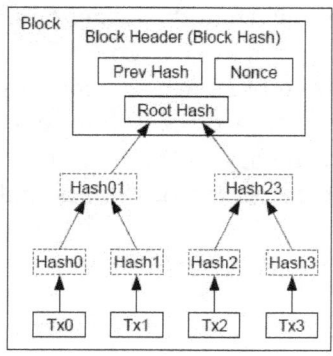

Transactions Hashed in a Merkle Tree

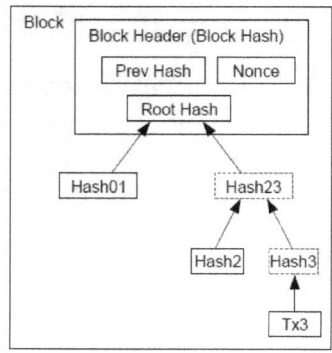

After Pruning Tx0-2 from the Block

A block header with no transactions would be about 80 bytes. If we suppose blocks are generated every 10 minutes, 80 bytes * 6 * 24 * 365 = 4.2MB per year. With computer systems typically selling with 2GB of RAM as of 2008, and Moore's Law predicting current growth of 1.2GB per year, storage should not be a problem even if the block headers must be kept in memory.

Simplified Payment Verification

It is possible to verify payments without running a full network node. A user only needs to keep a copy of the block headers of the longest proof-of-work chain, which he can get by querying network nodes until he's convinced he has the longest chain, and obtain the Merkle branch linking the transaction to the block it's time stamped in. He can't check the transaction for himself, but by linking it to a place in the chain, he can see that a network node has accepted it,
and blocks added after it further confirm the network has accepted it.

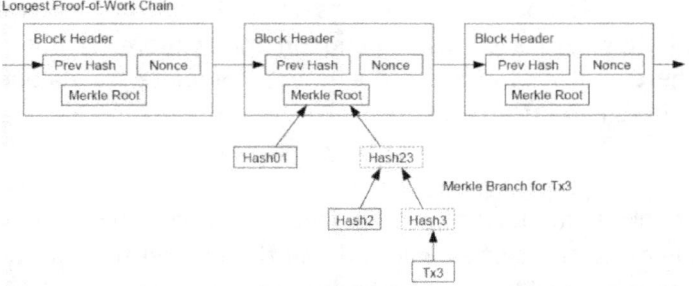

As such, the verification is reliable as long as honest nodes control the network, but is more vulnerable if the network is overpowered by an attacker. While network nodes can verify transactions for themselves, the simplified method can be fooled by an attacker's fabricated transactions for as long as the attacker can continue to overpower the network. One strategy to protect against this would be to accept alerts from network nodes when they detect an invalid block, prompting the user's software to download the full block and alerted transactions to confirm the inconsistency. Businesses that receive frequent payments will probably still want to run their own nodes for more independent security and quicker verification.

Combining and Splitting Value
Although it would be possible to handle coins individually, it would be unwieldy to make a separate transaction for every cent in a transfer. To allow value to be split and combined, transactions contain multiple inputs and outputs. Normally there will be either a single input from a larger previous transaction or multiple inputs combining smaller amounts, and at most two outputs: one for the payment, and one returning the change, if any, back to the sender.

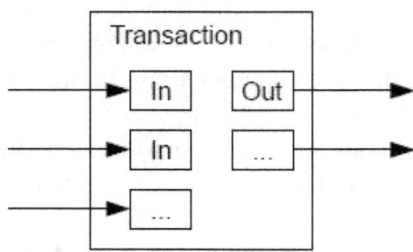

It should be noted that fan-out, where a transaction depends on several transactions, and those transactions depend on many more, is not a problem here. There is never the need to extract a complete standalone copy of a transaction's history.

Privacy
The traditional banking model achieves a level of privacy by limiting access to information to the parties involved and the trusted third party. The necessity to announce all transactions publicly precludes this method, but privacy can still be maintained by breaking the flow of information in another place: by keeping public keys anonymous. The public can see that someone is sending an amount to someone else, but without information linking the transaction to anyone. This is similar to the level of information released by stock exchanges, where the time and size of individual trades, the "tape", is made public, but without telling who the parties were.

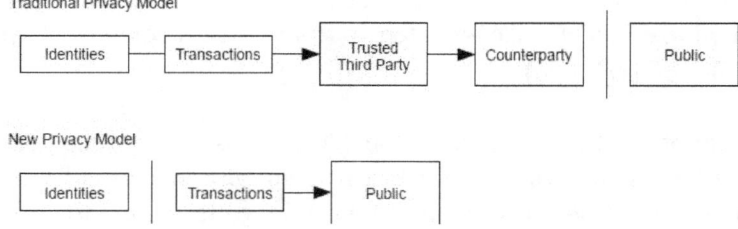

As an additional firewall, a new key pair should be used for each transaction to keep them from being linked to a common owner. Some linking is still unavoidable with multi-input transactions, which necessarily reveal that their inputs were owned by the same owner. The risk is that if the owner of a key is revealed, linking could reveal other transactions that belonged to the same owner.

Calculations

We consider the scenario of an attacker trying to generate an alternate chain faster than the honest chain. Even if this is accomplished, it does not throw the system open to arbitrary changes, such as creating value out of thin air or taking money that never belonged to the attacker. Nodes are not going to accept an invalid transaction as payment, and honest nodes will never accept a block containing them. An attacker can only try to change one of his own transactions to take back money he recently spent.

The race between the honest chain and an attacker chain can be characterized as a Binomial Random Walk. The success event is the honest chain being extended by one block, increasing its lead by +1, and the failure event is the attacker's chain being extended by one block, reducing thegap by -1.

The probability of an attacker catching up from a given deficit is analogous to a Gambler's Ruin problem. Suppose a gambler with unlimited credit starts at a deficit and plays potentially an infinite number of trials to try to reach breakeven. We can calculate the probability he ever reaches breakeven, or that an attacker ever catches up with the honest chain, as follows [8]:

p = probability an honest node finds the next block

q = probability the attacker finds the next block
qz = probability the attacker will ever catch up from z blocks behind

$$q_z = \begin{cases} 1 & \text{if } p \leq q \\ (q/p)^z & \text{if } p > q \end{cases}$$

Given our assumption that $p > q$, the probability drops exponentially as the number of blocks the attacker has to catch up with increases. With the odds against him, if he doesn't make a lucky lunge forward early on, his chances become vanishingly small as he falls further behind. We now consider how long the recipient of a new transaction needs to wait before being sufficiently certain the sender can't change the transaction. We assume the sender is an attacker who wants to make the recipient believe he paid him for a while, and then switch it to pay back to himself after some time has passed. The receiver will be alerted when that happens, but the sender hopes it will be too late.

The receiver generates a new key pair and gives the public key to the sender shortly before signing. This prevents the sender from preparing a chain of blocks ahead of time by working on it continuously until he is lucky enough to get far enough ahead, then executing the transaction at that moment. Once the transaction is sent, the dishonest sender starts working in secret on a parallel chain containing an alternate version of his transaction.

The recipient waits until the transaction has been added to a block and z blocks have been linked after it. He doesn't know the exact amount of progress the attacker has made, but assuming the honest blocks took the average expected time per block, the attacker's potential progress will be a Poisson distribution with expected value:

$$\lambda = z \frac{q}{p}$$

To get the probability the attacker could still catch up now, we multiply the Poisson density for each amount of progress he could have made by the probability he could catch up from that point:

$$\sum_{k=0}^{\infty} \frac{\lambda^k e^{-\lambda}}{k!}$$

$$\cdot \begin{cases} (q/p)^{z-k} & \text{if } k \leq z \\ 1 & \text{if } k > z \end{cases}$$

Rearranging to avoid summing the infinite tail of the distribution...

$$1 - \sum_{k=0}^{z} \frac{\lambda^k e^{-\lambda}}{k!} \left(1 - (q/p)^{z-k}\right)$$

Converting to C code...

```
#include <math.h>
double AttackerSuccessProbability(double q, int z)
{
    double p = 1.0 - q;
    double lambda = z * (q / p);
    double sum = 1.0;
    int i, k;
    for (k = 0; k <= z; k++)
    {
        double poisson = exp(-lambda);
        for (i = 1; i <= k; i++)
            poisson *= lambda / i;
        sum -= poisson * (1 - pow(q / p, z - k));
    }
    return sum;
}
```

Running some results, we can see the probability drop off exponentially with z.

```
q=0.1
z=0  P=1.0000000
z=1  P=0.2045873
z=2  P=0.0509779
z=3  P=0.0131722
z=4  P=0.0034552
z=5  P=0.0009137
z=6  P=0.0002428
z=7  P=0.0000647
z=8  P=0.0000173
```

z=9 P=0.0000046
z=10 P=0.0000012
q=0.3
z=0 P=1.0000000
z=5 P=0.1773523
z=10 P=0.0416605
z=15 P=0.0101008
z=20 P=0.0024804
z=25 P=0.0006132
z=30 P=0.0001522
z=35 P=0.0000379
z=40 P=0.0000095
z=45 P=0.0000024
z=50 P=0.0000006
Solving for P less than 0.1%...
P < 0.001
q=0.10 z=5
q=0.15 z=8
q=0.20 z=11
q=0.25 z=15
q=0.30 z=24
q=0.35 z=41
q=0.40 z=89
q=0.45 z=340

Recommendation

The Ethereum protocol was originally conceived as an upgraded version of a cryptocurrency, providing advanced features such as on-blockchain escrow, withdrawal limits and financial contracts, gambling markets and the like via a highly generalized programming language. The Ethereum protocol would not
"support" any of the applications directly, but the existence of a Turing-complete programming language means that arbitrary contracts can theoretically be created for any transaction type or application. What is more interesting about Ethereum, however, is that the Ethereum protocol moves far beyond just currency. Protocols and decentralized applications around decentralized file storage, decentralized computation and decentralized prediction markets, among dozens of other such concepts, have the potential to substantially increase the efficiency of the computational industry, and provide a massive boost to other peer-to-

peer protocols by adding for the first time an economic layer. Finally, there is also a substantial array of applications that have nothing to do with money at all.

The concept of an arbitrary state transition function as implemented by the Ethereum protocol provides for a platform with unique potential; rather than being a closed-ended, single-purpose protocol intended for a specific array of applications in data storage, gambling or finance, Ethereum is open-ended by design, and we believe that it is extremely well-suited to serving as a foundational layer for a very large number of both financial and non-financial protocols in the years to come.

The Swap protocol serves a growing demand for a decentralized asset exchange on the Ethereum network. Blockchain-based order books, while novel and certainly within the ethos of our ecosystem, have limitations that we believe ultimately make it di_cult for them to compete with currently available centralized solutions. Swap provides a method that is both decentralized and una_ected by these limitations.

By implementing the protocol, participants gain access to liquidity in a scalable, private, and fair way, without sacri_cing access to great pricing. The protocol and APIs are extensible and we encourage the community to build applications with us. We welcome feedback and look forward to pushing the Ethereum community forward with you.

Conclusion
We have proposed a system for electronic transactions without relying on trust. We started with the usual framework of coins made from digital signatures, which provides strong control of ownership, but is incomplete without a way to prevent double-spending. To solve this, we proposed a peer-to-peer network using proof-of-work to record a public history of transactions that quickly becomes computationally impractical for an attacker to change if honest nodes control a majority of CPU power. The network is robust in its unstructured simplicity. Nodes work all at once with little coordination. They do not need to be identified, since messages are not routed to any particular place and only need to be delivered on a best effort basis. Nodes can leave and rejoin the network at will, accepting the proof-of-work chain as proof of what happened while they were gone. They vote with their CPU power, expressing their acceptance of valid blocks by working on extending them and rejecting invalid blocks

by refusing to work on them. Any needed rules and incentives can be enforced with this consensus mechanism.

Although Ethereum and Bitcoin may have similar aspects the two currencies are very different in regards to the use and future of the two digital assets. While the future of Ethereum is uncertain there is an attractive investment opportunity to capture the potential gains of the technology. As for Bitcoin, there is still room for growth and value, but it will not be at the volatile rate it experienced in the beginning years.

www.ingramcontent.com/pod-product-compliance
Lightning Source LLC
Chambersburg PA
CBHW070258230526
45470CB00002B/630